Creative DIY Room Sprays

Natural Fragrances, Easy Recipes, and Tips for a Fresh, Inviting Home

NIGEL MUNDEN

COPYRIGHT

Copyright © [2025] by [Nigel Munden]
All rights reserved. No part of this publication may be reproduced, distributed, or transmitted in any form or by any means, including photocopying, recording, or other electronic or mechanical methods, without the prior written permission of the publisher, except in the case of brief quotations embodied in critical reviews and certain other noncommercial uses permitted by copyright law.

DEDICATION

To everyone who seeks to fill their home with the beauty of nature, one spritz at a time. May these simple, homemade room sprays bring peace, comfort, and a fresh, fragrant atmosphere to your everyday life.

And to my family and friends, whose love and support always inspire my creativity and passion—thank you for encouraging me to follow my dreams.

TABLE OF CONTENTS

COPYRIGHT
DEDICATION
TABLE OF CONTENTS
INTRODUCTION
 Why DIY Room Sprays? The Benefits of Homemade Fresheners
  2. Personalization
  3. Cost-Effective
  4. Environmentally Friendly
  5. Aromatherapy Benefits
  6. Avoiding Harsh Chemicals
  7. Fun and Creative
 How to Use This Book for a Fragrant Home
  Step-by-Step Instructions
  Tools and Ingredients
  Customization Tips
  Health and Safety Guidelines
  Troubleshooting and Tips
  Bonus Ideas
Chapter 1
Understanding Room Sprays
 What Are Room Sprays and How Do They Work?
  The Basics of Room Sprays
  Types of Room Sprays
  How Room Sprays Eliminate Odors
  How the Scent is Dispersed

Why Room Sprays Work So Well
The Role of Essential Oils in Room Sprays
Key Ingredients in Natural Room Sprays
   1. Water: The Base of Your Room Spray
      Why It's Important:
   2. Alcohol: For Dissolving Oils and Quick Evaporation
      Why It's Important:
   3. Essential Oils: The Heart of Your Room Spray
      Common Essential Oils and Their Benefits:
      Why They're Important:
   4. Glycerin (Optional): For Longer-Lasting Scent
      Why It's Important:
   5. Witch Hazel (Optional): For Extra Stability
      Why It's Important:
   6. Baking Soda (Optional): For Odor Neutralization
      Why It's Important:
   7. Natural Colorants (Optional): For Visual Appeal
      Why It's Important:
Common Benefits of Using DIY Sprays Over Commercial Ones
   1. Healthier and Safer for You and Your Family
      Common Harmful Chemicals in Commercial Sprays:
   2. Personalization and Customization

How Customization Works:
3. Control Over Ingredients
  Key Ingredients You Control:
4. Eco-Friendly and Sustainable
  How DIY Room Sprays Are More Eco-Friendly:
5. Cost-Effective in the Long Run
  How DIY Room Sprays Save You Money:
6. Therapeutic Benefits and Aromatherapy
  Examples of Therapeutic Benefits:
7. No Harsh or Overpowering Scents
  How DIY Sprays Offer a Better Scent Experience:
8. Fun and Creative Process
  Why DIY Sprays Are Fun:

Chapter 2
The Essential Tools You'll Need
  Bottles, Containers, and Storage Tips
    1. Choosing the Right Bottle
    2. Size of the Bottle
    3. Storage Tips
  Measuring and Mixing Tools
    1. Measuring Tools
    2. Mixing Tools
    3. Funnel
  Labeling and Personalizing Your Sprays
    1. Labeling Your Bottles
    2. Personalizing Your Room Sprays
  Conclusion: Preparing for Success

6

Chapter 3
The Science Behind Fragrance Blending
    Understanding Essential Oils and Their Properties
        What Are Essential Oils?
        Properties of Essential Oils
        Popular Essential Oils and Their Benefits:
    How to Mix Scents for Different Moods
        1. The Art of Blending Scents
        2. Blending for Different Moods
    Safe Guidelines for Using Essential Oils
        1. Dilution is Key
        2. Patch Test
        3. Avoiding Sensitive Areas
        4. Use with Caution Around Pets and Children
        5. Keep Oils Out of Reach

Chapter 4
Creative Recipes for Every Room
    Fresh Citrus Breeze (For Kitchens)
        Why Choose Citrus Scents for the Kitchen?
        Ingredients for Fresh Citrus Breeze Spray
        How to Make the Fresh Citrus Breeze Room Spray
        How to Use Fresh Citrus Breeze Spray
    Why This Works
    Tips for Personalizing Your Citrus Breeze Spray

- Relaxing Lavender & Chamomile (For Bedrooms)
    - Why Choose Lavender and Chamomile for the Bedroom?
        - Lavender: A Calming Powerhouse
        - Chamomile: A Gentle Soother
    - Ingredients for Relaxing Lavender & Chamomile Room Spray
    - How to Make the Relaxing Lavender & Chamomile Room Spray
    - How to Use Relaxing Lavender & Chamomile Room Spray
    - Why This Works
    - Tips for Personalizing Your Lavender & Chamomile Spray
- Uplifting Eucalyptus Mint (For Living Rooms)
    - Why Choose Eucalyptus and Mint for the Living Room?
        - Eucalyptus: Refreshing and Purifying
        - Peppermint: Energizing and Stimulating
    - Ingredients for Uplifting Eucalyptus Mint Room Spray
    - How to Make the Uplifting Eucalyptus Mint Room Spray
    - How to Use Uplifting Eucalyptus Mint Room Spray
    - Why This Works
    - Tips for Personalizing Your Uplifting Eucalyptus Mint Spray
- Refreshing Garden Blend (For Bathrooms)
    - Why Choose a Garden-Inspired Blend for the Bathroom?
        - Lemon: Bright, Clean, and Energizing

      Lavender: Floral and Calming
      Rosemary: Herbaceous and Purifying
      Geranium: Fresh and Floral
   Ingredients for Refreshing Garden Blend Room Spray
   How to Make the Refreshing Garden Blend Room Spray
   How to Use Refreshing Garden Blend Room Spray
   Why This Works
   Tips for Personalizing Your Refreshing Garden Blend Spray
Cozy Cinnamon & Clove (For Fall and Winter)
   Why Choose Cinnamon and Clove for Fall and Winter?
      Cinnamon: Warm, Spicy, and Inviting
      Clove: Rich, Spicy, and Festive
   Ingredients for Cozy Cinnamon & Clove Room Spray
   How to Make the Cozy Cinnamon & Clove Room Spray
   How to Use Cozy Cinnamon & Clove Room Spray
   Why This Works
   Tips for Personalizing Your Cozy Cinnamon & Clove Spray
Chapter 5
Customizing Your Room Sprays
   How to Adjust Scents for Personal Preferences
      Understanding the Basic Scent Profiles
         1. Floral Scents

2. Citrus Scents
3. Spicy Scents
4. Woody Scents
5. Herbal Scents
6. Sweet Scents
Adjusting Fragrance Strength
   1. More Subtle Fragrance:
   2. Stronger Fragrance:
Creating Seasonal Blends
   Fall/Winter Blends:
   Spring/Summer Blends:
   Holiday Blends:
Customizing for Different Rooms
   For the Kitchen:
   For the Living Room:
   For the Bathroom:
   For the Bedroom:
   For the Office or Study Room:
Final Tips for Customizing Your Room Spray
Experimenting with Different Combinations
   Unleashing Your Creativity with Essential Oils
   Starting with Basic Combinations
      1. Single-Scent Focus
      2. Complementary Blends
      3. Layered Blends
   Exploring Advanced Blending Techniques
      1. Combining Different Scent Families
      2. Layering for Different Moods
      3. Adjusting for Seasonal Scents

Testing and Refining Your Blends
1. Test in Small Batches
2. Let It Rest
3. Fine-Tuning
Customizing Scents for Specific Rooms
Adding Natural Color and Texture (Herbs, Dried Flowers)
Enhancing Your Room Sprays with Natural Elements
Why Add Herbs and Dried Flowers to Room Sprays?
1. Aesthetic Appeal
2. Gentle Fragrance Enhancement
3. Therapeutic Benefits
4. Eco-Friendly and Sustainable
Choosing the Right Herbs and Flowers for Your Room Spray
1. Lavender
2. Rose Petals
3. Rosemary
4. Chamomile
5. Hibiscus
6. Peppermint Leaves
7. Jasmine
How to Incorporate Herbs and Dried Flowers into Your Room Sprays
1. Infusion Method
2. Direct Placement
3. Herbal Oil Infusion
Creating a DIY Herb and Flower Room Spray Recipe

Lavender & Rose Petal Room Spray
Caring for Your Herbal & Floral Room Spray
Chapter 6
Tips for Long-Lasting Scents
How to Make Your Room Spray Last Longer
1. Choose the Right Base Ingredients
A. Use Alcohol or Witch Hazel as a Base
B. Use Distilled Water
2. Add Fixatives to Enhance Longevity
A. Glycerin
B. Sandalwood or Cedarwood Essential Oil
C. Orris Root Powder
3. Store Your Room Spray Properly
A. Store in Dark, Cool Places
B. Use Airtight Containers
4. Shake Well Before Each Use
5. Use Less Water, More Essential Oils
A. Essential Oil Concentration
B. Stronger Fragrances
6. Choose the Right Environment for Use
A. Spray in Small Doses
B. Airflow Considerations
C. Use Room Sprays When the Room is Still
7. Avoid Common Mistakes That Shorten the Life of Scents
A. Using Too Much Water
B. Not Using a Fixative

Storage and Care for Homemade Sprays
- How to Properly Store and Maintain Your DIY Room Sprays
  - 1. Store Your Room Sprays in Dark Glass Bottles
    - Why Use Dark Glass Bottles?
    - When to Use Clear Bottles
    - Tip:
  - 2. Store Room Sprays in Cool, Dry Places
    - Temperature Considerations
    - Humidity Levels
    - Best Storage Areas
  - 3. Seal Your Room Sprays Tightly
    - Airtight Seal
    - Tip:
  - 4. Shake Your Spray Before Each Use
    - Why Shake?
    - Tip:
  - 5. Use Room Sprays Within a Reasonable Time Frame
    - Shelf Life of Homemade Room Sprays
    - Signs Your Room Spray Has Gone Bad
    - Tip:
  - 6. Clean Your Spray Bottles Regularly
    - Why Clean Your Bottles?
    - How to Clean Your Spray Bottles
  - 7. Consider Adding Preservatives (Optional)
    - Why Add Preservatives?
    - Tip:
- Using Room Sprays to Enhance Your Environment

How Room Sprays Can Transform Your Space
   1. Setting the Mood with Fragrance
      A. Relaxing and Calming
      B. Uplifting and Energizing
      C. Focus and Productivity
   2. Creating Ambiance for Specific Rooms
      A. Bedroom: Rest and Relaxation
      B. Living Room: Inviting and Refreshing
      C. Kitchen: Clean and Invigorating
      D. Bathroom: Clean and Fresh
   3. Seasonal Scents for Special Occasions
      A. Fall and Winter
      B. Spring and Summer
   4. Using Room Sprays to Improve Air Quality
      A. Antibacterial and Antiviral Properties
      B. Neutralizing Odors
   5. Enhancing Your Experience with Room Sprays
      A. For Meditation and Yoga
      B. For Entertaining and Social Gatherings

Chapter 7
Eco-Friendly and Sustainable DIY Sprays
   Choosing Natural Ingredients
      1. Essential Oils: A Natural Powerhouse
         A. Why Choose Essential Oils?
         B. Popular Eco-Friendly Essential Oils
         Tip: When buying essential oils, always check for certifications like organic or wildcrafted to ensure you're getting the

purest, most sustainable option.
2. Carrier Oils: Supporting and Diluting Essential Oils
   A. Choosing the Right Carrier Oil
   Tip: Whenever possible, choose certified organic carrier oils and other natural liquids to ensure your DIY spray remains eco-friendly and non-toxic.
3. Hydrosols and Floral Waters: Eco-Friendly Alternatives
   A. Benefits of Hydrosols
   B. Popular Hydrosols to Use in Room Sprays
4. Sustainable Additives and Herbs
   A. Dried Herbs
   B. Other Additives
5. Packaging and Sustainability
   A. Glass Bottles
   B. Eco-Friendly Labels
   C. Refill Stations and Bulk Buying

Avoiding Harsh Chemicals and Preservatives
1. Common Chemicals to Avoid in Room Sprays
   A. Synthetic Fragrances
   B. Preservatives and Antimicrobials
   C. Alcohols and Solvents
2. The Benefits of Going Chemical-Free

Packaging Options for Eco-Conscious DIYers
1. Glass Bottles: The Sustainable Choice
   A. Benefits of Glass Bottles
   B. Types of Glass Bottles for Room

Sprays
    C. Where to Find Glass Bottles
2. Aluminum Bottles: Durable and Recyclable
    A. Benefits of Aluminum Bottles
    B. Types of Aluminum Bottles
    C. Where to Find Aluminum Bottles
3. Recycled Plastic Bottles
    A. Benefits of Recycled Plastic Bottles
    B. Where to Find Recycled Plastic Bottles
4. Sustainable Labeling Options
    A. Paper-Based Labels
    B. Water-Based Adhesives
5. Other Eco-Friendly Packaging Ideas
    A. Cloth Bags or Pouches
    B. Wooden Caps
6. Tips for Sustainable Packaging Practices

Chapter 8
Troubleshooting Common Issues
    Why Your Spray Isn't Lasting Long
    1. Incorrect Ratio of Essential Oils to Carrier Liquid
        A. How to Get the Right Balance
    2. Using the Wrong Carrier Liquid
        A. Why Water Might Not Be Enough
        B. Alternative Carrier Liquids to Consider
    3. Exposure to Heat and Sunlight
        A. Why Heat and Sunlight Matter

16

    B. How to Protect Your Room Spray
  4. The Wrong Type of Essential Oils
    A. Essential Oils That Evaporate Quickly
    B. Essential Oils That Last Longer
    C. Blending Oils for Longevity
  5. Overuse of Fragrance
    A. How Overuse Affects Longevity
    B. Finding the Right Scent Strength
  6. Poor Mixing Techniques
    A. Tips for Proper Mixing
  7. The Scent Isn't Strong Enough
    A. Increasing Scent Intensity
Fixing Overpowering Scents
  1. Dilution: The Easiest Fix for an Overpowering Scent
    A. How to Dilute Your Room Spray
    B. What to Consider When Diluting
  2. Adjusting the Blend of Oils
    A. How to Fix the Blend
    B. Experimenting with Ratios
  3. Allowing the Spray to Settle
    A. Let It Age
    B. Test and Adjust Over Time
  4. Use Less Frequent Spraying or Smaller Amounts
    A. How to Adjust Your Spraying Technique
Adjusting for Allergies or Sensitivities
  1. Identifying Potential Irritants
    A. Essential Oils to Avoid for Sensitive

Individuals
      2. Choosing Gentle Oils
         A. Hypoallergenic Essential Oils
      3. Reducing the Concentration of Essential Oils
         A. Adjusting the Ratio
      4. Test the Spray on Small Areas
         A. Testing in a Small Room or Area
      5. Choose Natural, Non-Toxic Ingredients
         A. Use 100% Pure Essential Oils
         B. Choose Non-Toxic Carrier Liquids
Chapter 9
Bonus Ideas for Room Spray Lovers
   Creative Gift Ideas Using Room Sprays
      1. Personalized Scented Gift Bottles
         A. Choosing the Perfect Scent
         B. Adding Personal Touches
      2. Aromatherapy Care Packages
         A. Essential Oils & Room Spray Pairing
         B. Packaging Ideas
      3. DIY Gift Sets for Special Occasions
         A. Holiday-Themed Gift Sets
         B. Wedding and Party Favors
      4. Aromatherapy Inhalers for On-the-Go
         A. Creating Aromatherapy Inhalers
      5. Room Spray Crafting Parties
         A. Hosting a Room Spray Crafting Party
   Seasonal Variations: DIY Sprays for Holidays and Special Occasions
      1. Spring Scents: Fresh and Floral

18

    A. Classic Floral Blends
    B. Citrus Burst
2. Summer Scents: Light and Energizing
    A. Tropical Paradise
    B. Fresh Mint & Eucalyptus
3. Fall Scents: Warm and Cozy
    A. Spiced Pumpkin
    B. Apple Cinnamon Delight
4. Winter Scents: Cozy and Inviting
    A. Holiday Spice
    B. Winter Wonderland
5. Special Occasions: Scents for Celebrations
    A. Wedding Day Bliss
    B. Birthday Bash

Making Room Spray Sets for Friends and Family

1. Choosing the Right Scents for Different People
    A. For the Relaxer: Calming and Soothing Scents
    B. For the Energizer: Fresh and Uplifting Scents
    C. For the Nature Lover: Earthy and Grounding Scents
2. Designing Your Room Spray Set
    A. Select Beautiful Bottles
    B. Personalize the Labeling
    C. Packaging and Presentation
3. Creating a Themed Room Spray Set
    A. Seasonal Theme
    B. Self-Care and Relaxation Theme

- C. Fresh & Clean Theme
  - 4. Adding a Personal Touch
- Conclusion
- Enjoying a Natural, Fragrant Home Every Day
  - Final Tips for Making the Most of Your DIY Room Sprays

INTRODUCTION

There's something special about walking into a room that smells fresh, inviting, and comforting. Whether you've just cleaned your home, or you simply want to brighten up the atmosphere, the power of fragrance is undeniable. Many of us reach for store-bought air fresheners or scented candles to achieve that pleasant aroma, but these options often come with unwanted chemicals, strong artificial scents, and hefty price tags.

This book is about empowering you to take control of the fragrances in your home by creating your own DIY room sprays. Not only will you be able to design scents that match your personal taste, but you'll also avoid harmful chemicals that can come with traditional commercial air fresheners. By the end of this book, you'll have everything you need to create natural, effective room sprays that can refresh your home, uplift your mood, and even enhance your well-being.

Why DIY Room Sprays? The Benefits of Homemade Fresheners

You may be wondering why you should take the time to create your own room sprays when store-bought options are readily available. Well, there are several compelling reasons to make your own sprays, and the benefits go beyond just having a pleasant smell.

1. Healthier Air Quality

Most commercial air fresheners contain synthetic chemicals that may emit toxins into the air, which can be harmful to your health. These chemicals may contribute to respiratory issues, skin irritation, and even headaches. With DIY room sprays, you control the ingredients, ensuring that you're only using natural, safe materials like essential oils and plant-based extracts.

2. Personalization

One of the best parts about making your own room sprays is the ability to create custom scents. If you love lavender or adore the crisp scent of eucalyptus, you can blend those essential oils to create the perfect fragrance for your space. DIY room sprays give you the freedom to experiment and find the right balance of scents for your home, matching your mood, the season, or even the occasion.

3. Cost-Effective

Store-bought air fresheners can be expensive, especially when you're constantly replenishing them. DIY room sprays are incredibly cost-effective. Essential oils and other ingredients can be bought in bulk and will last for many batches of room sprays. A few drops of essential oil can go a long way, making DIY sprays a wallet-friendly option in the long run.

4. Environmentally Friendly

Many commercial air fresheners come in plastic bottles and non-recyclable packaging, contributing to waste. By making your own room sprays, you can choose sustainable packaging options, such as glass spray bottles, and reduce your environmental footprint. You can also select natural, biodegradable ingredients, further supporting eco-conscious living.

5. Aromatherapy Benefits

Certain essential oils have therapeutic properties that can positively impact your mood, mind, and even your health. For example, lavender is known for its calming and stress-relieving effects, while citrus oils can boost energy and focus. By creating your own room sprays, you can tailor the scent to suit your emotional or physical needs, turning your home into a natural aromatherapy haven.

6. Avoiding Harsh Chemicals

Many commercial room sprays use phthalates, parabens, and other chemicals to prolong shelf life or enhance the fragrance. These ingredients can be harmful to both your health and the environment. DIY room sprays let you avoid these harsh chemicals, giving you peace of mind knowing you're using pure, natural ingredients.

7. Fun and Creative

Making your own room sprays is a fun and creative activity that allows you to experiment with different scents and combinations. You can get as creative as you like, and once you've perfected your favorite blends, you'll feel proud knowing you created something special for your home. Whether you're doing it as a hobby or to gift your friends and family, the process is enjoyable and fulfilling.

How to Use This Book for a Fragrant Home

This book is designed to be an easy-to-follow guide that will take you step by step through the process of creating your own room sprays. Whether you're a beginner or someone with some experience in DIY projects, you'll find everything you need here.

Step-by-Step Instructions

Each chapter provides clear, detailed instructions on how to create different types of room sprays. The recipes are simple and beginner-friendly, with tips for customization along the way. We've broken down the process to make it as straightforward as possible, so you can start making your own room sprays right away.

Tools and Ingredients

In the beginning chapters, we'll explain what tools and ingredients you'll need. You don't need a lot of specialized equipment, just some basic supplies that are easy to find at local stores or online. Each recipe also includes information about where to source the best ingredients and how to get the most out of them.

Customization Tips

Not all rooms are the same, and neither are all scent preferences. In this book, you'll learn how to adjust each recipe based on your preferences, whether you want a stronger fragrance or a more subtle scent. You'll also find guidance on how to blend different essential oils and other ingredients to create unique combinations tailored to your taste.

Health and Safety Guidelines

As you create your DIY room sprays, you'll want to be mindful of safety. Some essential oils are not recommended for certain conditions or around pets. This book will provide you with important safety guidelines to make sure you're using these ingredients properly and safely. We will also guide you on proper storage and how to prevent any mishaps while working with essential oils.

Troubleshooting and Tips

We've included a section dedicated to troubleshooting, where we address common problems you may encounter when making or using your room sprays. If your scent fades too quickly, if the spray isn't lasting as long as you'd like, or if you have trouble blending oils, we've got solutions for you.

Bonus Ideas

Towards the end of the book, you'll find bonus sections filled with creative ideas, such as how to make room spray gifts, seasonal variations, and eco-friendly options for packaging. These ideas will not only help you expand your DIY collection but also show you how to share the joy of natural fragrances with others.

By following this book, you'll be able to create your own natural, homemade room sprays and enjoy the many benefits they bring. From improving the air quality to boosting your mood with aromatherapy, this DIY approach to home fragrance will help transform your space into a haven of fresh, pleasant scents.

Chapter 1

Understanding Room Sprays

In this chapter, we'll cover the basics of room sprays—what they are, how they work, and the benefits they offer. Understanding these concepts is the first step toward creating your own effective DIY room sprays. Let's explore the science behind them and why they're such a great addition to any home.

What Are Room Sprays and How Do They Work?

Room sprays, also known as air fresheners or room fresheners, are liquid solutions designed to mask or eliminate unpleasant odors in your living space while adding a pleasant fragrance. Unlike candles or incense, which rely on heat or combustion to release their scent, room sprays rely on simple chemical principles to diffuse fragrance into the air.

The Basics of Room Sprays

At their core, room sprays are a blend of water, alcohol, and essential oils or other fragrance compounds. These ingredients are mixed together in specific proportions to create a solution that can be sprayed into the air. The primary goal of room sprays is to release aromatic molecules into the air that interact with our olfactory receptors (the sensors in our noses that detect smells), which our brain interprets as pleasant or unpleasant scents.

Here's how they work in simple terms:

- **Water** forms the base of the spray and serves as a solvent to dilute the essential oils.
- **Alcohol** helps the oils dissolve into the water and also aids in quick evaporation once the spray is applied. It also acts as a preservative to prevent bacterial growth in the solution.
- **Essential Oils** or synthetic fragrances are the key ingredients that create the scent. When you spray the solution into the air, the fragrance molecules are released and carried by the air currents, allowing them to be detected by your nose.

Types of Room Sprays

There are two primary types of room sprays: **natural** and **synthetic**.

- **Natural Room Sprays**: These are typically made using essential oils, which are concentrated extracts from plants. Essential oils are the heart of natural room sprays, and they provide not only fragrance but also therapeutic benefits. For example, lavender oil is calming, eucalyptus is refreshing, and lemon is energizing. Natural room sprays are favored for their health benefits and eco-friendliness, as they avoid synthetic chemicals and artificial fragrances.

- **Synthetic Room Sprays**: These sprays often use artificial fragrance compounds, which are cheaper to produce and offer a wider range of scents. However, many synthetic fragrances contain harmful chemicals like phthalates, parabens, and formaldehyde, which can contribute to indoor air pollution and may cause allergic reactions in some people.

How Room Sprays Eliminate Odors

Room sprays don't just mask odors—they can actually neutralize them. Here's how they work:

- **Odor Masking**: Many room sprays work by simply covering up bad smells with a more pleasant fragrance. For example, a floral room spray can cover up the scent of stale air or food odors. However, this only addresses the problem temporarily.

- **Odor Neutralizing**: Certain ingredients, such as essential oils, contain molecules that can bind to odor-causing particles, neutralizing them. For instance, citrus oils like lemon or orange have naturally strong, clean scents that can bind with the odor molecules in the air and render them neutral. Some sprays also contain other ingredients like vinegar or baking soda that can help absorb odors directly.

How the Scent is Dispersed

When you spray a room freshener into the air, the liquid droplets break into tiny particles that remain suspended in the air for a period of time. These tiny scent particles drift throughout the room, and as they make contact with your nose, they trigger your olfactory receptors, which send signals to the brain that interpret the smell.

The speed at which the scent disperses depends on factors like:

- **The type of alcohol used**: Alcohol helps the fragrance evaporate quickly, so you can smell the fragrance almost immediately after spraying.
- **Air circulation**: A well-ventilated room or a room with fans will help the fragrance disperse faster, making the scent more noticeable.
- **Humidity and Temperature**: Warmer temperatures and higher humidity can make fragrances evaporate more quickly, whereas cooler, drier conditions may cause scents to linger longer.

Why Room Sprays Work So Well

Room sprays work because they engage multiple senses—your sense of smell, your emotional responses, and even your memories. The power of scent is closely tied to emotions and memories. A pleasant smell can trigger positive emotions, such as relaxation, happiness, or nostalgia, while an unpleasant smell can create discomfort or stress. When you create your own DIY room sprays, you not only control the scent but also create an environment that fits your mood and enhances your emotional well-being.

In addition to improving your home's atmosphere, certain scents have therapeutic effects:

- **Lavender** can reduce stress and promote relaxation.
- **Peppermint** can boost energy and improve focus.
- **Lemon or citrus** scents are uplifting and energizing.

The Role of Essential Oils in Room Sprays

Essential oils play a central role in room sprays. These concentrated plant extracts provide not only fragrance but also a range of therapeutic properties that benefit your health and well-being. Each essential oil has a unique profile, and when blended together, they can enhance the overall scent experience.

Here's a quick overview of a few popular essential oils commonly used in room sprays:

- **Lavender**: Calming and relaxing, great for bedrooms or spaces where you want to create a peaceful atmosphere.
- **Peppermint**: Energizing and invigorating, perfect for workspaces or bathrooms.
- **Eucalyptus**: Refreshing and clean, helps to clear the air and can promote better breathing.
- **Lemon**: Bright, fresh, and energizing, ideal for kitchens or living spaces.
- **Tea Tree**: Antibacterial and purifying, often used in spaces that need a little extra freshening up.

By understanding how room sprays work and the role of essential oils, you're already well on your way to crafting your own blends that not only smell amazing but also support your well-being.

Key Ingredients in Natural Room Sprays

Creating natural room sprays requires a selection of key ingredients that are safe, effective, and easy to work with. These ingredients not only help deliver a pleasant fragrance but also ensure that your DIY room sprays are free from harsh chemicals and synthetic fragrances. In this chapter, we'll break down the essential components that make up natural room sprays, and why each one is important for creating a high-quality, natural product.

1. Water: The Base of Your Room Spray

Water is the primary base for any room spray. It serves as the carrier for all other ingredients and helps dilute the essential oils, which are concentrated and highly potent. Water also helps in dispersing the oils into the air when sprayed, ensuring an even distribution of the fragrance.

Why It's Important:

- **Dilutes Essential Oils**: Essential oils are too strong to be used undiluted, and water provides the necessary balance to make the spray safe for use.
- **Evaporation**: Water helps the solution evaporate into the air, ensuring that the fragrance lingers in the room.
- **Non-Toxic**: Water is safe, natural, and environmentally friendly, making it an ideal base ingredient for your room sprays.

2. Alcohol: For Dissolving Oils and Quick Evaporation

In natural room sprays, alcohol—often **vodka** or **isopropyl alcohol**—plays an essential role. It acts as a solvent for the essential oils, helping them dissolve into the water. Alcohol also aids in the quick evaporation of the fragrance once the spray is applied.

Why It's Important:

- **Solvent for Essential Oils**: Essential oils need to be blended properly with the base, and alcohol helps them mix effectively with water.
- **Quick Evaporation**: Alcohol evaporates quickly when sprayed into the air, which ensures that the fragrance is immediately noticeable without lingering too long in one place.
- **Preservation**: Alcohol acts as a natural preservative, preventing the growth of bacteria and mold, which can sometimes occur in water-based solutions.
- **No Strong Scent**: Vodka, for example, is odorless and will not overpower the fragrance of the essential oils.

3. Essential Oils: The Heart of Your Room Spray

Essential oils are the cornerstone of natural room sprays. These oils are derived from plants, flowers, herbs, and fruits, and they provide the scent and therapeutic properties for your spray. Essential oils not only freshen the air but also offer a range of benefits, including stress relief, energy boosts, and mood elevation.

Common Essential Oils and Their Benefits:

- **Lavender**: Calming and soothing, great for promoting relaxation, sleep, and stress relief.
- **Peppermint**: Refreshing and invigorating, helpful for increasing focus, energy, and even relieving headaches.
- **Lemon**: Uplifting and refreshing, known for its mood-boosting qualities and its ability to purify the air.
- **Eucalyptus**: Clean and fresh, often used for its ability to clear nasal passages and promote easy breathing.
- **Tea Tree**: Purifying and antibacterial, great for spaces that need extra freshening or when you want to reduce germs in the air.
- **Orange**: Sweet, warm, and cheerful, orange oil is uplifting and perfect for creating a cozy, happy atmosphere.

Why They're Important:

- **Customizable Scents**: Essential oils allow you to create your own unique fragrance blends, tailored to your personal preferences.
- **Therapeutic Properties**: Beyond just scent, essential oils can have positive effects on your health and mood, from calming anxiety (lavender) to boosting concentration (peppermint).
- **Natural and Safe**: Unlike synthetic fragrances, essential oils are natural and chemical-free,

offering a safer alternative for both your health and the environment.

4. Glycerin (Optional): For Longer-Lasting Scent

Glycerin is a natural compound that helps your room spray last longer. It is an optional ingredient, but it can be added to the mixture to increase the longevity of the fragrance by making it more viscous and helping it cling to surfaces a bit longer.

Why It's Important:

- **Prolongs Scent**: Glycerin helps slow down the evaporation of essential oils, allowing the fragrance to last longer in the room.
- **Moisturizing**: Glycerin is often used in skincare products because of its moisturizing properties, and it can help hydrate the air, creating a fresher environment.
- **Non-Toxic**: It's safe for both humans and pets, making it a great addition to a non-toxic room spray.

5. Witch Hazel (Optional): For Extra Stability

Witch hazel is a natural astringent that can be used as an alternative to alcohol. It helps dissolve essential oils into the water and provides additional shelf stability. While it may not evaporate as quickly as alcohol, it's still effective in room sprays.

Why It's Important:

- **Non-Evaporating**: Witch hazel doesn't evaporate as quickly as alcohol, meaning your room spray may have a slightly longer-lasting fragrance when applied.
- **Soothing**: Witch hazel is known for its soothing properties, which can be helpful if you're using room sprays in sensitive areas like bedrooms or around children.
- **Natural and Gentle**: Witch hazel is a natural, plant-based ingredient that offers a gentle way to bind oils to water without the stronger scent of alcohol.

6. Baking Soda (Optional): For Odor Neutralization

Baking soda is a powerful natural odor neutralizer. While it's not an ingredient that is commonly used in room sprays, it can be included in some recipes for its ability to absorb and neutralize unpleasant smells. It's especially useful in rooms with pet odors or musty smells.

Why It's Important:

- **Neutralizes Odors**: Baking soda traps odor molecules, helping to eliminate unwanted smells in your space.

- **Natural and Safe**: It's non-toxic and safe for pets and children, making it an excellent option for natural cleaning and freshening.
- **Affordable**: Baking soda is a very cost-effective way to improve the efficacy of your room spray without adding any chemicals.

---

7. Natural Colorants (Optional): For Visual Appeal

If you want to make your DIY room sprays more visually appealing, you can add a few drops of natural colorants. Ingredients like **beetroot powder**, **spirulina**, or **herbal teas** can add a splash of color to your room spray without compromising its natural composition.

Why It's Important:

- **Aesthetic Appeal**: Adding natural colorants can make your room sprays look more attractive, especially if you plan to give them as gifts.
- **Customizable**: Color can also reflect the mood or fragrance of the spray. For instance, a calming lavender spray might feature a soft purple hue, while a refreshing citrus blend could have a yellow or green tint.

Now that you understand the key ingredients that go into natural room sprays, you're ready to start experimenting with your own blends. Each ingredient serves a specific purpose—whether it's to dilute, dissolve, or provide the therapeutic effects of essential oils.

As you create your DIY room sprays, remember that you can adjust the proportions of water, alcohol, essential oils, and optional ingredients based on your preferences and desired effects. The beauty of making your own sprays is that you have full control over the ingredients, ensuring that your room sprays are as natural and personalized as you want them to be.

Common Benefits of Using DIY Sprays Over Commercial Ones

When it comes to room sprays, many people reach for the familiar, store-bought options without thinking twice. Commercial air fresheners and sprays are widely available and promise instant results. However, the benefits of making your own DIY room sprays go far beyond simply saving money. In this chapter, we'll explore the advantages of using homemade sprays compared to commercial ones, from the health benefits to the customizability of scents.

1. Healthier and Safer for You and Your Family

One of the biggest reasons people switch to DIY room sprays is the health aspect. Many commercial room fresheners contain harmful chemicals that can negatively impact your health over time. These chemicals can irritate your skin, eyes, and respiratory system, and some have even been linked to more serious health conditions. On the other hand, DIY room sprays are made with natural ingredients, providing a much safer alternative.

Common Harmful Chemicals in Commercial Sprays:

- **Phthalates**: Often used in fragrances, phthalates have been linked to hormone disruption and reproductive issues.

- **Formaldehyde**: Found in many air fresheners, formaldehyde is a known carcinogen and can irritate the skin, eyes, and respiratory system.
- **Parabens**: These are preservatives used in commercial sprays, but they can disrupt the endocrine system and affect hormone balance.

By using DIY room sprays made with simple, natural ingredients like essential oils, alcohol, and water, you avoid exposure to these toxic chemicals and create a healthier environment for yourself and your family.

---

2. Personalization and Customization

Another standout benefit of DIY room sprays is the ability to personalize and create a scent that's perfectly tailored to your tastes. Commercial sprays usually offer a limited range of fragrances—often overly sweet or artificial. With DIY sprays, you can create any scent combination you desire by blending different essential oils to suit your preferences.

How Customization Works:

- **Personal Preferences**: Whether you love floral, citrus, herbal, or woodsy scents, you can choose your favorite essential oils and combine them in a way that's unique to you.
- **Mood-Based Scents**: Want a calming fragrance for your bedroom? Use lavender and chamomile. Need an energizing scent for your workspace? Try a blend of citrus and peppermint. With DIY room sprays, the possibilities are endless.

- **Seasonal Variations**: You can create room sprays that fit the mood of the season—think spicy cinnamon for winter, fresh lemon for summer, or earthy cedarwood for fall.

---

3. Control Over Ingredients

Commercial room sprays are often packed with preservatives, artificial fragrances, and chemical stabilizers, many of which you may not want in your home. When you make your own sprays, you have complete control over the ingredients, ensuring they are safe, natural, and tailored to your needs.

Key Ingredients You Control:

- **Essential Oils**: Choose from a wide range of oils, each with its own benefits—whether you're looking for something relaxing like lavender or something refreshing like eucalyptus.
- **Alcohol and Water**: These base ingredients are simple, safe, and customizable. You can adjust their quantities to control the strength and evaporation rate of your spray.
- **No Hidden Chemicals**: By making your own room sprays, you avoid any harmful additives, knowing exactly what's in each bottle.

4. Eco-Friendly and Sustainable

Environmental impact is another major benefit of DIY room sprays. Commercial air fresheners are typically sold in plastic bottles, and the production of these bottles, as well as the chemicals inside, can have a negative environmental footprint. Making your own sprays allows you to significantly reduce waste and contribute to a more sustainable lifestyle.

How DIY Room Sprays Are More Eco-Friendly:

- **Reusable Containers**: DIY room sprays often use glass or reusable plastic spray bottles, which can be refilled over and over. This helps reduce the need for single-use plastic.
- **Natural Ingredients**: Many essential oils are derived from plants and can be produced sustainably, without the need for harmful chemicals or processes.
- **Reduced Packaging**: By buying ingredients in bulk and using minimal packaging, you reduce overall waste.

5. Cost-Effective in the Long Run

While making DIY room sprays may have a slightly higher upfront cost (due to the purchase of essential oils and other ingredients), over time, it's much more cost-effective than buying commercial sprays regularly. A small bottle of essential oil can last for many batches of room spray, and the basic ingredients like water and alcohol are very inexpensive.

How DIY Room Sprays Save You Money:

- **Long-Term Use**: A few drops of essential oil can go a long way, meaning you only need to buy oils once in a while.
- **Bulk Buying**: Many of the ingredients used in DIY room sprays, such as alcohol or witch hazel, can be purchased in bulk, saving you money in the long run.
- **No Need for Frequent Purchases**: Since you can make a batch of room spray that lasts for months, you won't have to buy replacements frequently, unlike commercial sprays that often run out quickly.

6. Therapeutic Benefits and Aromatherapy

Commercial room sprays often focus only on masking odors, with little thought given to the potential benefits of scent beyond just fragrance. DIY room sprays, on the other hand, offer a range of therapeutic advantages, thanks to the essential oils they contain. Essential oils can promote relaxation, reduce stress, improve focus, and even boost your immune system.

Examples of Therapeutic Benefits:

- **Lavender**: Known for its calming and sleep-inducing properties, lavender is perfect for reducing anxiety and promoting restful sleep.
- **Peppermint**: Great for boosting energy and concentration, peppermint oil can help you stay alert and focused throughout the day.

- **Eucalyptus**: Known for its ability to clear nasal passages and promote easy breathing, eucalyptus is ideal for cold and flu seasons.
- **Lemon and Citrus**: These oils are energizing, uplifting, and often used to improve mood and focus.

With DIY room sprays, you get the added bonus of aromatherapy, which can have both physical and emotional benefits.

7. No Harsh or Overpowering Scents

Many commercial room sprays contain synthetic fragrances that can be overwhelming or have a harsh, chemical undertone. DIY room sprays, on the other hand, offer a more subtle and natural scent experience. When you make your own sprays, you can adjust the strength of the fragrance to suit your preferences, ensuring a light, pleasant scent that won't overpower the room.

How DIY Sprays Offer a Better Scent Experience:

- **Customizable Strength**: You can control how strong or light you want the fragrance to be by adjusting the amount of essential oil.
- **Natural Fragrance**: The scents from essential oils are much more pleasant and natural, giving your home a fresh, authentic aroma without the harshness of artificial chemicals.

8. Fun and Creative Process

Making your own DIY room sprays can be a fun and creative activity. It's a great way to explore different scent combinations, experiment with various essential oils, and craft something unique. Whether you're creating sprays for yourself, your family, or as gifts for others, the process itself can be deeply rewarding.

Why DIY Sprays Are Fun:

- **Creative Experimentation**: Mixing different oils and ingredients lets you experiment with various scent combinations and learn what works best for you.
- **Gift-Giving**: DIY room sprays make wonderful, personal gifts for friends and family. You can tailor the scent to the recipient's preferences or create something that fits a special occasion, like a seasonal scent for the holidays.

The benefits of DIY room sprays are clear: they're healthier, customizable, cost-effective, eco-friendly, and offer a more natural, therapeutic experience. By making your own room sprays, you gain control over the ingredients and the fragrance, ensuring that your home smells just the way you want it—without any of the negative side effects of commercial air fresheners.

Chapter 2

The Essential Tools You'll Need

Creating your own DIY room sprays can be a fun and rewarding project, but to achieve the best results, having the right tools on hand is crucial. In this chapter, we'll go over all the essential equipment you'll need to get started, from the bottles you'll store your sprays in to the tools you'll use for measuring and mixing. Additionally, we'll discuss labeling and personalizing your sprays so that they not only smell great but also look great and are easy to identify.

Bottles, Containers, and Storage Tips

The right bottle or container for your DIY room sprays plays an important role in both the effectiveness and shelf life of your final product. From selecting the appropriate size to ensuring that your spray bottle is functional and eco-friendly, here's what you need to consider when choosing the perfect container.

1. Choosing the Right Bottle

- **Spray Bottles**: The most common type of container for DIY room sprays is a **spray bottle**. These allow for an even and controlled distribution of the fragrance when sprayed into the air. Look for bottles that have a **fine mist spray nozzle** to ensure that the solution is dispersed evenly throughout the room.

- **Material**: Most DIY room sprays are stored in either **glass** or **plastic** bottles. Each has its pros and cons:
    - **Glass Bottles**: Glass is the ideal choice for long-term storage because it's non-reactive, so your room spray won't interact with the material. It's also more eco-friendly since glass is recyclable and reusable. However, glass bottles are heavier and more prone to breakage, so they may not be the best option if you're planning to carry your spray around.
    - **Plastic Bottles**: Plastic is lighter and less fragile, which is great if you plan on keeping your spray bottle in different areas of the home. However, be cautious of low-quality plastics that may interact with essential oils and degrade over time. It's recommended to choose **PET plastic** bottles, which are durable and safe for essential oils.

2. Size of the Bottle

- **Small Bottles (2-4 oz)**: Perfect for personal use or when you're testing out different scent blends. Small bottles are easy to store and convenient to carry with you, especially if you want to make small batches of room spray.
- **Medium Bottles (6-8 oz)**: These are ideal if you're creating room sprays for regular use around the house or for gifting. They provide

enough room for multiple applications without taking up too much space.
- **Large Bottles (16 oz or more)**: Larger bottles are great if you plan to make large batches of room spray for use in several rooms or for gifting purposes. They're also a more cost-effective option if you use room sprays frequently.

3. Storage Tips

- **Store in a Cool, Dark Place**: Essential oils can degrade when exposed to heat and light, so it's important to store your room spray in a cool, dark location. A cabinet or drawer is ideal.
- **Avoid Direct Sunlight**: UV rays can break down the oils and cause your spray to lose its potency over time. Ensure your bottles are stored away from direct sunlight to preserve the fragrance.
- **Shelf Life**: DIY room sprays that contain water can last between 1 to 3 months. Adding alcohol or witch hazel as a preservative can extend the shelf life. Keep track of the date you made each spray, and toss it if it starts to look cloudy or smells off.

Measuring and Mixing Tools

While you don't need to invest in specialized equipment for making DIY room sprays, having the right measuring and mixing tools makes the process much easier and more accurate. Here are the basic tools you'll need:

1. Measuring Tools

- **Measuring Cups**: A small **liquid measuring cup** (typically 1 to 2 cups) is essential for accurately measuring water, alcohol, and witch hazel. For best results, use a cup with clear measurement markings to avoid guesswork.
- **Teaspoons/Tablespoons**: For essential oils and other smaller quantities, a **teaspoon** or **tablespoon** is your best tool. These come in handy when adding small amounts of oils, glycerin, or other optional ingredients.
- **Syringe or Dropper**: Essential oils are potent, and you only need a few drops at a time. Using a **dropper** or **syringe** will help you measure essential oils precisely, so your fragrance isn't too overpowering or too weak.

2. Mixing Tools

- **Glass or Stainless Steel Mixing Bowls**: For larger batches of room spray, a small **mixing bowl** can be helpful to blend your ingredients before transferring them to your spray bottle. Opt for glass or stainless steel to avoid any chemical reactions with the oils.
- **Whisk or Stirrer**: A **small whisk** or **stirring stick** is great for mixing the ingredients thoroughly. Essential oils don't naturally dissolve in water, so a good stir ensures that the oils blend well before adding them to the bottle.

3. Funnel

- **Funnel**: A **funnel** will help you pour your room spray into the bottle without spilling. This is especially important when transferring liquids from a mixing bowl to a small spray bottle. A small, plastic funnel with a narrow opening is perfect for this task.

Labeling and Personalizing Your Sprays

Personalizing your DIY room sprays adds a professional touch, especially if you're gifting them or selling them. A well-designed label not only makes your spray look appealing but also helps you keep track of the ingredients, scent combinations, and the creation date.

1. Labeling Your Bottles

- **Materials for Labels**: You can create labels using **sticker paper**, **chalkboard labels**, or even **pre-printed labels** that you can find at office supply stores. Make sure to choose a label material that can withstand light moisture exposure, as your room spray bottle will likely get wet during use.
- **Information to Include**:
    - **Scent Name**: Give your room spray a creative name or label it based on its primary scent (e.g., "Lavender Dream" or "Citrus Burst").
    - **Ingredients**: Include a simple list of the ingredients used in the spray, such as "Lavender Essential Oil, Vodka, Water," for transparency, especially if gifting or selling.
    - **Date Created**: Writing the date the room spray was made will help you track how long it has been since you made it. This can be especially helpful

51

when determining when it's time to replace it.
- **Usage Instructions**: A brief note on how to use the spray and a reminder to shake the bottle before each use is a nice touch. For example, "Shake well before spraying to mix oils."

2. Personalizing Your Room Sprays

- **Decorative Labels**: You can personalize your labels with decorative elements, like botanical illustrations or fun fonts, to give your room sprays a unique and charming appearance. There are many online design tools like **Canva** where you can create your own label designs for free.
- **Adding Color**: If you want to go the extra mile, add a little **natural colorant** (like beet juice, spirulina powder, or a drop of food coloring) to your spray. Be sure to use a safe, natural colorant, and don't overdo it—just a drop or two will give it a lovely hue.
- **Gift-Worthy Touch**: If you're making sprays for gifts, consider adding a decorative ribbon or tag with a personal message. This elevates the experience for the recipient and makes it feel special.

Conclusion: Preparing for Success

Having the right tools and equipment is crucial when making DIY room sprays. Whether you're mixing up a refreshing lavender spray or a citrus-infused air freshener, using the right bottles, measuring tools, and labels will ensure that your sprays are both functional and beautiful. By taking the time to personalize and properly store your creations, you can enjoy your DIY sprays for longer and even share them with friends and family.

Chapter 3

The Science Behind Fragrance Blending

Creating a room spray isn't just about mixing a few ingredients together; it's a carefully crafted art that combines the power of scent with the benefits of aromatherapy. In this chapter, we will explore the science behind fragrance blending, focusing on essential oils, their properties, and how to mix them effectively. You'll also learn how to create scents that evoke specific moods, along with safe guidelines for using essential oils, ensuring your blends are both safe and effective.

Understanding Essential Oils and Their Properties

Essential oils are the heart and soul of most DIY room sprays. These concentrated plant extracts contain the natural fragrances and therapeutic properties of the plants from which they are derived. Understanding the different types of essential oils and their properties will help you choose the right oils for your specific needs, whether you're aiming to relax, energize, or refresh the air.

What Are Essential Oils?

Essential oils are volatile compounds extracted from plants through distillation or cold pressing. The oil contains the "essence" of the plant's scent and its therapeutic properties. For example, lavender essential oil is known for its calming and sleep-inducing qualities, while peppermint oil is invigorating and uplifting.

Properties of Essential Oils

Each essential oil has distinct properties that can affect the mind and body in different ways. Some oils have calming effects, while others are stimulating or purifying. Here are some common properties of essential oils:

- **Relaxing/Calming**: Oils like lavender, chamomile, and sandalwood are known for their ability to promote relaxation, reduce stress, and improve sleep quality.
- **Energizing/Stimulant**: Citrus oils like lemon, orange, and grapefruit, as well as peppermint and eucalyptus, are invigorating and can help clear the mind and increase focus.
- **Antiseptic/Cleansing**: Oils such as tea tree, eucalyptus, and thyme have natural antibacterial and antiviral properties, making them great for purifying the air.
- **Mood Lifting**: Oils like rose, ylang-ylang, and jasmine are known for their uplifting properties, improving mood and creating an atmosphere of warmth and positivity.
- **Grounding**: Oils like frankincense, patchouli, and vetiver have earthy, grounding qualities that can help with emotional stability and focus.

Popular Essential Oils and Their Benefits:

- **Lavender**: Calms anxiety, improves sleep, and promotes relaxation.
- **Peppermint**: Relieves headaches, energizes, and improves focus.
- **Lemon**: Uplifts mood, promotes focus, and has antibacterial properties.
- **Eucalyptus**: Clears the airways, has purifying properties, and helps with concentration.
- **Tea Tree**: Antibacterial, antiviral, and antifungal properties, ideal for cleansing the air.
- **Rosemary**: Stimulates the mind, improves memory, and has antibacterial qualities.

Understanding the different properties of essential oils will allow you to create blends that not only smell delightful but also deliver the intended therapeutic benefits.

How to Mix Scents for Different Moods

One of the most exciting aspects of creating your own room sprays is the ability to craft specific scents that can influence the atmosphere of any room. Whether you want to create a relaxing environment in your bedroom or a refreshing atmosphere in your kitchen, fragrance blending is an art that can be learned and mastered with practice.

1. The Art of Blending Scents

When blending essential oils for a room spray, it's essential to understand the concept of "notes." Just like in music, scents have different layers that blend together to create a harmonious fragrance profile. These layers are categorized into **top**, **middle**, and **base** notes:

- **Top Notes**: These are the first scents you'll smell when you spray the room spray. They are usually light, fresh, and volatile, evaporating quickly. Common top notes include citrus oils like lemon and orange, as well as minty oils like peppermint.

- **Middle Notes**: These are the heart of the fragrance and are typically more robust and lingering than top notes. Middle notes help to balance the lighter top notes and provide depth to the scent. Examples of middle notes are lavender, rosemary, and geranium.

- **Base Notes**: Base notes are the foundation of your fragrance. These oils are heavier, slower to evaporate, and often linger in the air long after the top and middle notes have dissipated. Base notes include earthy, woody, and spicy oils like sandalwood, patchouli, and frankincense.

2. Blending for Different Moods

Now that you understand the basics of scent notes, let's explore how to mix them to create blends that evoke specific moods or emotions.

- **Relaxation and Stress Relief**:
    - **Lavender + Chamomile + Sandalwood**

- - Lavender is an excellent choice for relaxation and stress relief, while chamomile helps calm the nerves and promote sleep. Adding a touch of sandalwood adds an earthy base note that grounds the blend, creating a soothing and calming environment.
- **Energy and Focus:**
  - Peppermint + Lemon + Rosemary
  - **Peppermint** stimulates the mind and increases focus, while **lemon** helps to uplift the spirit. **Rosemary** adds an earthy, refreshing note that enhances concentration. This blend is perfect for workspaces or study areas.
- **Mood Uplifting and Positivity:**
  - Orange + Ylang Ylang + Geranium
  - **Orange** is bright and cheerful, making it great for lifting the mood. **Ylang-ylang** adds a floral sweetness that promotes emotional well-being, and **geranium** balances the blend with a hint of floral freshness.
- **Calming Sleep Aid:**
  - Lavender + Bergamot + Frankincense
  - A classic blend for a peaceful night's sleep, **lavender** promotes relaxation, **bergamot** relieves stress, and **frankincense** offers a grounding, calming base note that enhances the sleep-inducing effects of the blend.
- **Fresh and Clean Atmosphere:**

- **Lemon + Eucalyptus + Tea Tree**
- **Lemon** offers a fresh and crisp scent, while **eucalyptus** clears the air and promotes mental clarity. **Tea tree** is purifying, making this blend great for kitchens or bathrooms where a fresh and clean atmosphere is desired.

Safe Guidelines for Using Essential Oils

Essential oils are incredibly powerful, and while they offer numerous benefits, they must be used carefully. Here are some important safety guidelines to follow when working with essential oils:

1. Dilution is Key

Essential oils are highly concentrated, so it's essential to dilute them properly before using them in room sprays or applying them to your skin. A general rule of thumb is to use **15-20 drops of essential oil** per **1 ounce of carrier liquid** (such as water, alcohol, or witch hazel) for a room spray. This ensures that the oil is safe to use and won't irritate your skin or cause discomfort.

2. Patch Test

Before using a new essential oil or a blend of oils, always do a **patch test** to check for skin sensitivities. Apply a small drop of the diluted essential oil to the inside of your wrist or elbow and wait 24 hours to see if any irritation occurs. This is particularly important if you plan to use the oils in a personal room spray (e.g., as a body spray).

3. Avoiding Sensitive Areas

Some essential oils can cause irritation if applied directly to sensitive areas like the eyes, mucous membranes, or broken skin. Always avoid spraying room sprays near your eyes or face, and never apply undiluted essential oils directly to your skin.

4. Use with Caution Around Pets and Children

Some essential oils can be harmful to pets, especially cats and dogs. Oils like **tea tree**, **eucalyptus**, and **citrus** oils can be toxic to animals when inhaled or ingested. Always check whether a particular essential oil is safe for use around pets. Additionally, when using essential oils around children, use only oils that are safe for their age group, and dilute them properly.

5. Keep Oils Out of Reach

Essential oils should be stored in a safe place, away from children and pets. These oils are potent, and small amounts can cause irritation or adverse reactions if ingested or mishandled.

Understanding essential oils and their properties, how to mix them for specific moods, and following safe guidelines will give you the tools to create effective and enjoyable room sprays. Whether you're blending oils to relax, energize, or purify, the right combination of scents can transform the atmosphere of your home.

Chapter 4

Creative Recipes for Every Room

Creating a room spray isn't just about mixing ingredients—it's about crafting a unique atmosphere that enhances the space you're in. In this chapter, we'll explore creative and refreshing room spray recipes for every room in your home. Each recipe is designed with specific areas in mind, taking into account the natural flow of energy and fragrance. Whether you want to energize your kitchen, calm your bedroom, or refresh your bathroom, there's a spray for every need.

Fresh Citrus Breeze (For Kitchens)

The kitchen is the heart of the home, where cooking, entertaining, and family time come together. However, it's also an area that can often become overwhelmed with food odors, from garlic and onions to fried foods and strong spices. A Fresh Citrus Breeze room spray is perfect for this space—it not only helps neutralize odors but also uplifts the atmosphere with bright, refreshing scents. Citrus oils are known for their ability to cleanse and invigorate, making them ideal for kitchens.

Why Choose Citrus Scents for the Kitchen?

Citrus scents, such as lemon, orange, and grapefruit, are naturally energizing and refreshing. They have strong antibacterial properties that help purify the air and reduce the spread of germs. Citrus oils also promote a sense of cleanliness and freshness, which is especially important in spaces like the kitchen where food odors can linger.

In addition to their purifying qualities, citrus oils are uplifting and mood-boosting. If you spend a lot of time in the kitchen cooking, a citrus-based room spray will make the space feel inviting and vibrant, creating a pleasant ambiance for both cooking and socializing.

Ingredients for Fresh Citrus Breeze Spray

- **1/2 cup distilled water**: The base for your room spray, helping to dilute the oils and spread the fragrance evenly.
- **1/4 cup witch hazel or vodka**: Acts as an emulsifier and helps the essential oils blend with the water. Witch hazel also has purifying properties, while vodka ensures the oils are evenly dispersed when you spray.
- **20 drops lemon essential oil**: A bright, fresh, and cleansing scent that purifies the air and cuts through any kitchen odors.
- **10 drops orange essential oil**: Uplifting and energizing, this oil adds a sweet, refreshing layer to the blend.
- **5 drops grapefruit essential oil**: Known for its refreshing and clarifying qualities, grapefruit oil adds a zesty kick that complements the citrus base.

How to Make the Fresh Citrus Breeze Room Spray

1. **Prepare Your Bottle:**
   - Choose a 4-oz. spray bottle (glass is preferable, but plastic works fine too). Rinse it out thoroughly to ensure it's clean and dry before use.

2. **Mix the Ingredients:**
   - Start by adding the **witch hazel or vodka** into your spray bottle. This will act as the carrier for the essential oils and help them mix with the water.
   - Next, drop in the **essential oils: 20 drops of lemon, 10 drops of orange**, and **5 drops of grapefruit**. You can adjust the quantities to suit your preferences, but this combination offers a balanced, energizing scent.
   - Fill the rest of the bottle with **distilled water**. Leave some room at the top so that you can shake the bottle without spillage.

3. **Shake and Mix:**
   - Screw the cap onto the bottle and shake it well to blend the oils and water. Since essential oils don't dissolve in water, a good shake before each use ensures that the oils are evenly dispersed. Shake the bottle again every time you use it.

4. **Test the Spray:**
   - Spray the room spray into the air, preferably in the kitchen where it can neutralize any odors. Take a moment to

enjoy the fresh, uplifting fragrance of the citrus oils. If you want a stronger scent, feel free to add a few more drops of essential oil to the mix.

How to Use Fresh Citrus Breeze Spray

- **In the Kitchen**: Spray it around your cooking area, especially after meal preparation, to eliminate lingering food odors. A few spritzes near the stove, sink, or trash can will help neutralize smells and leave the kitchen smelling fresh.
- **On Fabrics**: If your kitchen curtains or towels tend to absorb food smells, you can lightly mist them with this spray to refresh them.
- **Before or After Guests Arrive**: A quick spritz in the kitchen before or after hosting guests can help create a clean, welcoming environment that's free of cooking smells. The citrus aroma will also energize your guests, adding to the overall positive atmosphere.

Why This Works

The combination of lemon, orange, and grapefruit oils offers a natural and effective way to freshen up your kitchen. Their bright, zesty aroma lifts the mood and clears the air, while the antibacterial properties help purify the environment. The witch hazel or vodka acts as a carrier and preservative, while the distilled water keeps the mixture light and non-oily.

Using a DIY room spray like **Fresh Citrus Breeze** is a cost-effective, eco-friendly way to ensure your kitchen always smells fresh, clean, and inviting. Plus, because it's made with essential oils, you avoid the toxic chemicals often found in commercial air fresheners. The added bonus? You can customize the recipe as you see fit—experiment with other citrus oils like lime or bergamot to create your own signature scent!

Tips for Personalizing Your Citrus Breeze Spray

If you'd like to add a personal touch to this recipe or adapt it for different uses, here are a few ideas:

- **Add Fresh Herbs**: For a more complex fragrance, add a few drops of **rosemary** or **thyme**. These herbs complement citrus scents and enhance the purifying qualities of the spray.
- **Adjust the Strength**: If you find the scent to be too strong or too light, adjust the number of drops of essential oil. For a more intense scent, increase the number of drops; for a lighter fragrance, reduce it.
- **Use a Blend of Citrus Oils**: Mix different citrus oils like **lime** or **mandarin** to create a unique fragrance that works best for you.

The **Fresh Citrus Breeze** room spray is a perfect way to keep your kitchen smelling clean, fresh, and inviting. The bright citrus scents not only help neutralize cooking odors but also uplift your mood and create an energizing atmosphere. Whether you're cooking, entertaining, or simply spending time in your kitchen, this easy-to-make room spray will ensure that the space always feels vibrant and pleasant.

Relaxing Lavender & Chamomile (For Bedrooms)

Your bedroom is more than just a place to sleep—it's your sanctuary, your escape, and your personal retreat. It's a space meant to promote rest, relaxation, and peace of mind. A room spray made with lavender and chamomile is perfect for creating a soothing environment that encourages calm and tranquility. The gentle, floral scents of these two essential oils are ideal for winding down after a long day and preparing your body and mind for a restful night's sleep.

In this section, we'll walk through a simple recipe for creating a **Relaxing Lavender & Chamomile Room Spray** that will help transform your bedroom into a peaceful oasis.

Why Choose Lavender and Chamomile for the Bedroom?

Lavender and chamomile are two of the most widely used essential oils for relaxation, and for good reason. They both offer a range of calming properties that can ease anxiety, promote deep sleep, and create an overall sense of well-being.

Lavender: A Calming Powerhouse

Lavender essential oil is one of the most popular oils for relaxation, known for its ability to soothe the nervous system and promote restful sleep. The scent of lavender has been scientifically proven to lower heart rate and blood pressure, reducing feelings of stress and anxiety. This makes it an ideal choice for the bedroom, where relaxation and calm are the main goals.

Lavender's gentle, floral aroma is both calming and comforting, perfect for unwinding after a busy day or creating a sleep-friendly atmosphere. It's also known for its antiseptic properties, making it a natural air purifier, which can help maintain the freshness of the bedroom.

Chamomile: A Gentle Soother

Chamomile has been used for centuries as a natural remedy for insomnia, anxiety, and muscle tension. Its gentle floral fragrance is a natural stress reliever, making it ideal for bedtime. Chamomile's calming properties work in harmony with lavender to promote relaxation and induce sleep, creating a peaceful environment perfect for unwinding and drifting into slumber.

Chamomile is also known for its anti-inflammatory properties, which can soothe the skin and help create a gentle, nurturing atmosphere in the bedroom. It's a great option if you're looking to create a warm, comforting, and inviting space.

Ingredients for Relaxing Lavender & Chamomile Room Spray

- **1/2 cup distilled water**: The main base of your room spray, helping to dilute the oils and ensure an even mist.
- **1/4 cup witch hazel or vodka**: This helps the oils to blend properly with the water and serves as an emulsifier, ensuring the oils don't separate.
- **20 drops lavender essential oil**: Lavender is the key ingredient that promotes relaxation, calm, and peaceful sleep.
- **10 drops chamomile essential oil**: Chamomile adds a layer of gentle calming to the blend, enhancing the soothing effects of lavender.
- **Optional: 5 drops bergamot essential oil**: If you want to add a citrusy twist to your blend, bergamot can help uplift the fragrance while still keeping the relaxing properties intact. It's particularly great for soothing anxiety and balancing mood.

How to Make the Relaxing Lavender & Chamomile Room Spray

1. **Prepare Your Spray Bottle**:
   - Choose a **4-ounce spray bottle** (preferably glass). Glass is ideal because it preserves the integrity of the essential oils over time.
   - Clean the bottle thoroughly before use to remove any dust or residue that might interfere with your spray.

2. **Add the Ingredients:**
   - Pour the **witch hazel or vodka** into your spray bottle. This will act as a carrier and ensure that the essential oils mix well with the water.
   - Add **20 drops of lavender essential oil** to the bottle. Lavender is the dominant note in this spray, so it will form the base of the fragrance.
   - Add **10 drops of chamomile essential oil** to enhance the relaxing, calming qualities.
   - If you're using **bergamot**, add **5 drops** to give the blend a subtle citrus twist that still complements the floral notes.
   - Fill the rest of the bottle with **distilled water**, leaving some space at the top to allow room for shaking.

3. **Shake the Bottle:**
   - Once all your ingredients are in the bottle, screw the cap on tightly and shake it well. Since essential oils don't naturally mix with water, shaking the bottle helps to disperse the oils evenly throughout the liquid.
   - Make sure to shake it every time before use to ensure the oils are properly emulsified.

4. **Test the Spray:**
   - Test the spray in your bedroom. Hold the bottle about 6-8 inches from the air and spritz lightly around the room. Take a deep breath and allow the calming

lavender and chamomile scents to fill the space. If you find the scent too subtle, you can add a few extra drops of essential oil to intensify the fragrance.

How to Use Relaxing Lavender & Chamomile Room Spray

- **Before Bedtime**: The most common use for this room spray is to help you relax before sleep. Spritz it lightly around the room, especially on your pillow or bed linens, to create a calm environment that encourages sleep.

- **Calming Environment**: If you're feeling anxious or stressed during the day, a quick spritz of this calming room spray can help to alleviate tension. Lavender and chamomile both have gentle, soothing properties that can create a peaceful atmosphere in any room.

- **On Your Bedding**: Mist your pillows and bed linens before going to sleep to create a serene, sleep-friendly environment. This spray is gentle and won't stain, making it perfect for fabric refreshment.

- **Room Refreshing**: If your bedroom feels stuffy or stale, a few spritzes of this refreshing lavender and chamomile spray will clear the air and promote relaxation. It's particularly great to use in bedrooms that don't get a lot of natural ventilation.

Why This Works

The combination of **lavender** and **chamomile** essential oils in this spray helps reduce stress, calm anxiety, and create an atmosphere of tranquility. Lavender's floral aroma is known to induce sleep, while chamomile complements this with its own gentle calming qualities. Together, they work in harmony to promote deep relaxation and a restful night's sleep.

By adding **witch hazel** or **vodka**, you're not only ensuring that the oils blend smoothly with the water, but you're also introducing additional purifying elements into the air. This combination makes your room spray an effective and safe alternative to chemical-laden air fresheners, which often contain artificial scents and harmful ingredients.

Tips for Personalizing Your Lavender & Chamomile Spray

If you'd like to customize the recipe to fit your preferences, here are a few variations you can try:

- **Add Ylang Ylang**: For a touch of sweetness, add **5 drops of ylang-ylang essential oil** to the blend. This oil promotes relaxation and enhances the calming effect of lavender and chamomile.

- **Use Dried Flowers**: If you want a more natural touch, you can add dried **lavender flowers** or **chamomile blossoms** into the bottle (before adding the liquid). This adds a visual appeal and reinforces the fragrance as the flowers release their natural oils over time.

- **Blend with Vanilla**: To create a warm, cozy ambiance, blend in a few drops of **vanilla essential oil**. It pairs wonderfully with the floral notes of lavender and chamomile for a sweet, calming atmosphere.

The **Relaxing Lavender & Chamomile Room Spray** is an essential addition to any bedroom. It combines the calming power of lavender and chamomile to create a soothing, peaceful environment perfect for winding down. Whether you use it nightly to help with sleep or whenever you need a moment of calm, this spray will help transform your bedroom into a restful sanctuary.

Uplifting Eucalyptus Mint (For Living Rooms)

The living room is the heart of the home, where relaxation, family bonding, and entertaining guests come together. It's a space where you want to feel comfortable, yet energized—inviting, yet refreshing. **Eucalyptus and mint** are two essential oils that perfectly capture this balance. They both have invigorating properties that clear the air and promote mental clarity, making them ideal for a living room environment.

An **Uplifting Eucalyptus Mint Room Spray** will not only refresh the air but also create a space that feels alive, clean, and vibrant. Whether you're hosting friends, relaxing with family, or simply enjoying some quiet time, this room spray will enhance the atmosphere, leaving you with a space that feels rejuvenated and fresh.

Why Choose Eucalyptus and Mint for the Living Room?

Both eucalyptus and mint are known for their stimulating and refreshing properties, making them an ideal combination for the living room.

Eucalyptus: Refreshing and Purifying

Eucalyptus essential oil is known for its invigorating and purifying qualities. It has a fresh, clean scent that promotes mental clarity and focus, which is perfect for a

74

living room that's often used for reading, conversation, or light activities. It also has antimicrobial properties, making it great for purifying the air and neutralizing any lingering odors.

Eucalyptus is a powerful, sharp scent that clears the airways and promotes a sense of freshness. When sprayed in the living room, it helps to eliminate stale odors, giving the space an overall feeling of cleanliness and energy.

Peppermint: Energizing and Stimulating

Mint, particularly peppermint, is an energizing essential oil that stimulates the senses. It's known for its cooling properties and ability to uplift the mood. The crisp, mentholated fragrance of peppermint can instantly refresh a room, making it feel more open and airy. Peppermint also has invigorating properties, promoting alertness and focus, which can be beneficial if you use your living room for activities that require attention, like reading or problem-solving.

Together, eucalyptus and mint create a fragrance blend that is both refreshing and mentally stimulating, perfect for revitalizing the atmosphere in your living room.

Ingredients for Uplifting Eucalyptus Mint Room Spray

- **1/2 cup distilled water**: The main carrier of the spray that helps dilute the essential oils and spread the fragrance evenly.

- **1/4 cup witch hazel or vodka**: Helps to emulsify the oils and blend them with the water, ensuring the spray doesn't separate.
- **20 drops eucalyptus essential oil**: This strong, refreshing oil purifies the air, promotes mental clarity, and adds a clean, crisp scent to the room.
- **15 drops peppermint essential oil**: Provides a cool, energizing aroma that boosts the air's freshness and promotes mental alertness.
- **Optional: 5 drops lemon essential oil**: For an added layer of brightness, you can include lemon essential oil. It will enhance the freshness of the eucalyptus and mint, giving the spray an extra burst of energy.

How to Make the Uplifting Eucalyptus Mint Room Spray

1. **Prepare Your Bottle**:
    - Select a **4-ounce spray bottle**, preferably made of glass. Glass preserves the integrity of the essential oils and doesn't interact with them.
    - Rinse the bottle thoroughly to ensure there's no dust or residue left behind.
2. **Mix the Ingredients**:
    - Start by adding the **witch hazel or vodka** into your spray bottle. This will help blend the oils with the water.
    - Add **20 drops of eucalyptus essential oil**, followed by **15 drops of peppermint essential oil**. If you want a

more citrusy kick, drop in **5 drops of lemon essential oil**.
- Fill the rest of the bottle with **distilled water**, leaving a bit of space at the top so you can shake the bottle without it overflowing.

3. **Shake the Bottle**:
    - Once all the ingredients are in the bottle, secure the cap and shake the mixture well to ensure the oils are properly blended with the water. Shake the bottle each time before use to keep the oils mixed.

4. **Test the Spray**:
    - Test the spray in your living room. Hold the bottle about 6-8 inches from the air and spray lightly into the room. The scent should be fresh, cool, and uplifting. If you find the fragrance too light or too strong, adjust the number of drops of essential oil as needed.

How to Use Uplifting Eucalyptus Mint Room Spray

- **In the Living Room**: The living room is where you entertain, relax, and engage in activities. A few spritzes of this uplifting room spray will create a lively, refreshing atmosphere. It's perfect for making the space feel open and invigorated.

- **For Entertaining**: If you're hosting guests or spending time with family, the combination of eucalyptus and mint will help clear the air, keeping the space feeling fresh and energizing. It also helps eliminate any lingering odors from cooking or other activities.

- **For Reading or Study Sessions**: If you use the living room as a study or reading space, the scent of eucalyptus and mint can help improve concentration and mental clarity. It's perfect for creating an alert, focused atmosphere.

- **Refreshing Stale Air**: If your living room feels stuffy or has a stale odor, a quick spritz of this room spray will refresh the air and create a vibrant, clean atmosphere.

Why This Works

The **Uplifting Eucalyptus Mint Room Spray** is the perfect solution for clearing the air and adding an energetic, fresh vibe to your living room. The combination of **eucalyptus** and **peppermint** essential oils works to purify the air, neutralize odors, and promote mental clarity. They're both known for their refreshing, invigorating properties, making them ideal for spaces that are meant to feel lively, open, and welcoming.

The **witch hazel** or **vodka** ensures the oils mix seamlessly with the water, while the **distilled water** acts as a neutral base, ensuring the scent is not overpowering.

Tips for Personalizing Your Uplifting Eucalyptus Mint Spray

- **Add Rosemary for Focus**: If you want to boost the mental clarity aspect of the spray, try adding **5 drops of rosemary essential oil**. Rosemary is known for its cognitive-enhancing properties and blends well with eucalyptus and mint.

- **Increase Citrus Notes**: If you enjoy a more citrus-forward scent, add **5 drops of orange essential oil** or **lime essential oil**. These oils will complement the cool, fresh notes of eucalyptus and mint, adding a zesty lift to the fragrance.

- **Adjust for Scent Strength**: Eucalyptus and mint have strong, vibrant fragrances, so adjust the number of drops based on your personal preference. If the scent is too overpowering, reduce the number of drops and see how the blend feels.

The **Uplifting Eucalyptus Mint Room Spray** is a perfect addition to your living room, especially if you want to create a refreshing, vibrant, and energizing atmosphere. Whether you use it to freshen the air after cooking or as a way to keep your space feeling alert and lively, this spray is the ideal solution for any time of day. It's a great way to cleanse the air, improve focus, and uplift the mood.

Refreshing Garden Blend (For Bathrooms)

The bathroom is a sanctuary of freshness and cleanliness, a place where you start and end your day. With its often enclosed space, it's important to maintain a pleasant atmosphere that eliminates odors while promoting a sense of relaxation and refreshment. A **Refreshing Garden Blend** room spray, crafted with natural essential oils, can transform your bathroom into a fragrant oasis, evoking the feeling of a blooming garden with every spritz.

The combination of **citrusy**, **herbaceous**, and **floral** scents in this blend makes it perfect for neutralizing bathroom odors while providing an uplifting, nature-inspired fragrance. Whether you're getting ready for the day or unwinding with a hot bath, this room spray will elevate your bathroom experience with the soothing scents of nature.

Why Choose a Garden-Inspired Blend for the Bathroom?

The bathroom is a space that often requires more frequent freshening due to humidity and other environmental factors. A garden-inspired room spray is perfect because it naturally neutralizes odors while introducing a light, refreshing atmosphere. Here's why certain essential oils are ideal for the bathroom:

Lemon: Bright, Clean, and Energizing

Lemon essential oil has a clean, crisp, and zesty fragrance that is well-known for its ability to purify and refresh the air. It has strong antibacterial properties that help eliminate unwanted odors in spaces like the bathroom. The uplifting nature of lemon also works to boost your mood and energize the senses, making it perfect for a quick burst of freshness first thing in the morning or after a relaxing bath.

Lavender: Floral and Calming

Lavender is one of the most versatile essential oils and is widely used for its soothing and relaxing properties. While it's often used in bedrooms for sleep, lavender is also great in the bathroom because of its ability to balance out stronger, sharper scents like lemon. Its floral notes help create a calming atmosphere, perfect for moments of relaxation in the bath or shower.

Rosemary: Herbaceous and Purifying

Rosemary essential oil has a strong herbal, pine-like fragrance that's ideal for cleansing the air and promoting a sense of clarity. It complements the refreshing properties of lemon while adding a unique depth to the scent. Rosemary's purifying qualities help eliminate lingering odors in the bathroom and provide a crisp, clean atmosphere.

Geranium: Fresh and Floral

Geranium essential oil has a sweet, floral fragrance that's reminiscent of a blooming garden. It's known for its ability to uplift the mood and promote emotional well-being. In combination with lavender and lemon, it helps create a balanced and harmonious fragrance blend that is both refreshing and relaxing.

Ingredients for Refreshing Garden Blend Room Spray

- **1/2 cup distilled water**: The base of your room spray, ensuring an even mist when you use it.
- **1/4 cup witch hazel or vodka**: Acts as an emulsifier to help the essential oils mix with the water and prevents them from separating.
- **15 drops lemon essential oil**: The crisp, clean scent of lemon purifies the air and adds a zesty freshness to the room.
- **10 drops lavender essential oil**: Adds a floral, calming note that balances the sharper, citrusy tones of the lemon.
- **10 drops rosemary essential oil**: Provides a fresh, herbaceous aroma that helps purify the air and complement the other oils.
- **Optional: 5 drops geranium essential oil**: For a floral, garden-like touch, geranium adds a pleasant sweetness that deepens the overall fragrance.

How to Make the Refreshing Garden Blend Room Spray

1. **Choose Your Spray Bottle**:
   - Select a **4-ounce glass spray bottle** for your room spray. Glass is ideal because

it doesn't affect the essential oils, helping preserve their fragrance and potency.

2. **Mix the Base Ingredients**:

   o Start by pouring **witch hazel or vodka** into the spray bottle. This ingredient helps the oils mix well with the water and ensures even distribution.

   o Add **15 drops of lemon essential oil** for a refreshing, energizing scent.

   o Follow with **10 drops of lavender essential oil**, which will create a calming balance and provide a floral note.

   o Add **10 drops of rosemary essential oil** to add an herbaceous, refreshing quality to the blend.

   o If you'd like to bring in a richer, floral garden element, add **5 drops of geranium essential oil**.

3. **Fill the Bottle with Water**:

   o Top up the spray bottle with **distilled water**, leaving a small gap at the top to allow for shaking.

4. **Shake and Mix**:

   o Once all the ingredients are in the bottle, secure the cap and shake the mixture well. This will help the oils blend with the water and ensure the scent is evenly distributed.

5. **Test the Spray**:

- Test the spray in your bathroom by lightly misting the air. The fragrance should feel fresh and rejuvenating. If the scent is too light, you can add a few more drops of the essential oils to intensify it.

How to Use Refreshing Garden Blend Room Spray

- **Before or After a Shower**: The refreshing blend of lemon, lavender, and rosemary makes this room spray perfect for the bathroom, especially after a shower or bath. A quick spritz will help freshen the air and provide a clean, uplifting atmosphere.

- **For Neutralizing Odors**: Bathrooms can sometimes hold onto unwanted smells. This spray helps neutralize those odors naturally and creates a fresh, pleasant scent that feels like walking into a garden.

- **In the Toilet Area**: Spraying a bit of the garden blend in the toilet area can help eliminate unwanted bathroom odors. Lemon's purifying qualities are great for this!

- **During Relaxing Bath Time**: If you're soaking in the tub, spritz the room with this refreshing blend to create a spa-like atmosphere. The lavender adds a calming note that enhances relaxation.

Why This Works

The **Refreshing Garden Blend Room Spray** works because it combines the best of nature's purifying, refreshing, and calming properties. **Lemon** clears the air and adds a clean, zesty fragrance, while **lavender** soothes and balances out the sharper scents. **Rosemary** helps purify the air, and **geranium** adds a layer of floral sweetness that rounds out the fragrance.

This blend is ideal for the bathroom, where freshness is essential. Whether you need to neutralize odors, freshen the air, or create a calming atmosphere, this room spray has it all. It's natural, non-toxic, and a much healthier alternative to commercial bathroom fresheners that often contain harmful chemicals.

Tips for Personalizing Your Refreshing Garden Blend Spray

- **Add Peppermint for Extra Freshness**: If you like an even more invigorating scent, add **5 drops of peppermint essential oil**. This will enhance the freshness of the blend and give it an extra cooling effect.

- **Try a Floral Twist with Ylang Ylang**: If you prefer a more floral note, **5 drops of ylang-ylang** can be added to the blend for a sweeter, more exotic fragrance.

85

- **Make It Citrus-Centric**: If you prefer citrus scents, you can up the ante by adding **orange essential oil** or **lime essential oil** to the mix. These oils bring a tangy, sweet freshness that works beautifully with the other ingredients.

The **Refreshing Garden Blend Room Spray** is a wonderful way to create a clean, fresh, and uplifting atmosphere in your bathroom. With its combination of **lemon**, **lavender**, and **rosemary**, this spray will neutralize odors, clear the air, and provide a revitalizing scent that feels like a walk through a blooming garden. Whether you're refreshing the space after a shower or looking to add a calming touch to your bath, this room spray is the perfect solution.

Cozy Cinnamon & Clove (For Fall and Winter)

As the cooler months roll in and the air takes on a crisp edge, there's nothing like the warm, comforting aroma of **cinnamon** and **clove** to set the mood for the season. These spices have been celebrated for centuries not just for their taste but for their ability to create a cozy, inviting atmosphere. A **Cozy Cinnamon & Clove Room Spray** is the perfect way to infuse your home with the essence of fall and winter, evoking feelings of warmth, comfort, and the delightful aroma of freshly baked goods.

Whether you're settling in for a cozy evening by the fire or preparing for family gatherings, this room spray adds an instant touch of seasonal cheer to any room. The combination of **spicy cinnamon** and **rich clove** creates a scent that's both comforting and festive, perfect for creating a homey, inviting atmosphere during the cooler months.

Why Choose Cinnamon and Clove for Fall and Winter?

The combination of **cinnamon** and **clove** essential oils is a powerful one for the fall and winter months. These oils have deep, spicy fragrances that are known for their warming properties. Together, they bring a sense of comfort and relaxation to your home, making them perfect for this time of year.

Cinnamon: Warm, Spicy, and Inviting

Cinnamon is one of the most beloved spices during the fall and winter seasons. Its warm, spicy aroma evokes thoughts of baking, hot drinks, and festive celebrations. **Cinnamon essential oil** not only creates an inviting, comforting environment, but it also has natural **antibacterial** and **antifungal** properties, which can help purify the air.

Cinnamon is also known for its ability to promote warmth and energy, making it ideal for the cooler months when you want to create a cozy atmosphere at home. Its rich, sweet, and spicy notes blend perfectly with clove to provide a comforting fragrance that fills the room.

Clove: Rich, Spicy, and Festive

Clove essential oil has a rich, warm, and spicy fragrance that complements cinnamon beautifully. It's often used in holiday blends because of its ability to create a festive atmosphere. Clove is known for its ability to neutralize odors and purify the air, making it perfect for use in the home during the colder months when indoor air tends to feel stale.

The **comforting aroma of clove** is deeply associated with winter celebrations and cozy evenings. It's grounding, soothing, and promotes relaxation, making it a great choice for evenings spent with family or a warm cup of tea.

Ingredients for Cozy Cinnamon & Clove Room Spray

- **1/2 cup distilled water**: The primary base for your spray, ensuring an even mist without leaving any residue.
- **1/4 cup witch hazel or vodka**: Helps emulsify the oils, ensuring that they mix well with the water and do not separate.
- **20 drops cinnamon essential oil**: Provides a warm, spicy, and inviting scent that's perfect for creating a cozy atmosphere.
- **15 drops clove essential oil**: Complements the cinnamon with its rich, warm fragrance and has purifying properties.
- **Optional: 10 drops orange essential oil**: Adds a touch of sweetness and a slight citrusy note to the blend, bringing a festive flair to the room spray.

How to Make the Cozy Cinnamon & Clove Room Spray

1. **Prepare Your Bottle**:
   - Choose a **4-ounce glass spray bottle** to ensure the essential oils remain intact and the fragrance is preserved.
   - Rinse the bottle with warm water to clean it thoroughly before use.
2. **Mix the Ingredients**:
   - Start by adding **witch hazel or vodka** to the bottle. This ingredient will help

blend the essential oils with the water, ensuring the oils are well-mixed and the scent is evenly distributed.
- Add **20 drops of cinnamon essential oil** to create the warm, spicy base of the fragrance.
- Follow with **15 drops of clove essential oil**, which will add richness and depth to the blend.
- For an extra festive touch, add **10 drops of orange essential oil** for a sweet, citrusy note that complements the spicy cinnamon and clove.

3. **Add Distilled Water:**
   - Fill the rest of the bottle with **distilled water**, leaving a little space at the top to allow for shaking and mixing.

4. **Shake and Mix:**
   - Secure the cap tightly and shake the bottle vigorously to ensure the essential oils blend well with the water and witch hazel. Shake the bottle each time before use to keep the oils mixed.

5. **Test the Spray:**
   - Spray a fine mist into the air, testing the fragrance in your space. It should immediately feel warm and cozy. If you feel the fragrance is too subtle, you can increase the number of essential oil drops to suit your preference.

How to Use Cozy Cinnamon & Clove Room Spray

- **For a Cozy Living Room**: Whether you're curled up on the couch with a blanket or hosting a family gathering, a few spritzes of this cozy blend will instantly transform the room into a warm, inviting space. The cinnamon and clove combination is perfect for those chilly nights when you want to feel at home and relaxed.

- **During Fall and Winter Holidays**: If you're preparing your home for a holiday gathering or family dinner, the **Cozy Cinnamon & Clove Room Spray** is perfect for filling the air with a festive, comforting fragrance. It's ideal for creating a holiday-ready atmosphere in your kitchen, living room, or dining area.

- **In the Bedroom for Restful Nights**: The rich, warm aroma of cinnamon and clove can also be used in the bedroom, especially during the colder months when you need help unwinding after a long day. The comforting scent promotes relaxation and sets the tone for a peaceful night's rest.

- **In the Kitchen After Cooking**: Kitchens often carry lingering cooking smells, especially during the holidays. A spritz of this room spray can help neutralize odors while creating a festive atmosphere. It's especially useful after baking holiday treats, as the scent of cinnamon and clove will mimic the aromas of fresh-baked pies.

Why This Works

The **Cozy Cinnamon & Clove Room Spray** works because it captures the essence of fall and winter with its combination of **cinnamon** and **clove**. Both oils have warming, purifying properties that help neutralize odors while creating a comforting, festive ambiance. Cinnamon provides an energizing, sweet-spicy scent, while clove adds depth and richness, making this spray perfect for creating a cozy home during the colder months.

Additionally, the optional **orange essential oil** adds a zesty, sweet note that rounds out the spicy blend, creating a fragrance that feels both festive and refreshing.

Tips for Personalizing Your Cozy Cinnamon & Clove Spray

- **Add a Touch of Vanilla**: If you want a sweeter, dessert-like fragrance, you can add **5 drops of vanilla essential oil** to your spray. The combination of vanilla with cinnamon and clove will evoke the scent of warm holiday treats like cinnamon rolls and cookies.

- **Boost with Nutmeg**: For a more complex, holiday-inspired fragrance, add **3 drops of nutmeg essential oil**. This will add a warm, spicy note that pairs wonderfully with cinnamon and clove.

- **Enhance with Pine**: If you want to evoke the fresh, woodsy scent of a Christmas tree, add **5 drops of pine essential oil**. The crispness of pine balances out the sweetness of cinnamon and clove, adding a fresh twist to the blend.

The **Cozy Cinnamon & Clove Room Spray** is the perfect addition to your home during the fall and winter months. Whether you're setting the mood for a holiday gathering, refreshing the air after cooking, or simply creating a cozy atmosphere for a quiet evening, this room spray delivers warmth, comfort, and the familiar scents of the season. The combination of **cinnamon**, **clove**, and optional **orange** creates a festive, inviting fragrance that fills your home with the spirit of fall and winter.

Chapter 5

Customizing Your Room Sprays

How to Adjust Scents for Personal Preferences

One of the most exciting parts of making your own DIY room sprays is the ability to create unique scents that truly reflect your personal preferences. Unlike commercial air fresheners, which often use artificial fragrances, DIY room sprays allow you to blend **essential oils** in ways that not only suit your space but also cater to your individual tastes and needs. Whether you prefer a more floral fragrance, a fresh and citrusy burst, or a warm, spicy atmosphere, the world of essential oils offers endless possibilities to customize your room sprays.

In this chapter, we'll guide you through the process of **adjusting scents** to suit your own preferences and even how to experiment with different combinations to create your own signature blend. We'll also explore how to balance the strength of a fragrance, adjust for the seasons, and make room sprays that work for specific rooms or occasions.

Understanding the Basic Scent Profiles

When customizing room sprays, it's essential to understand the different **scent families** or **profiles** that essential oils fall into. These scent families have distinct characteristics that allow you to combine oils that balance and complement each other perfectly. Here's a brief overview of the main scent profiles:

1. Floral Scents

Floral essential oils are often associated with relaxation, beauty, and calm. These oils tend to be sweet and aromatic, with a natural softness. Examples include:

- **Lavender**
- **Geranium**
- **Rose**
- **Ylang Ylang**
- **Jasmine**

Floral scents are great for bedrooms and bathrooms, creating a peaceful and serene atmosphere.

2. Citrus Scents

Citrus oils are light, bright, and energizing. They can also have a refreshing quality that's perfect for kitchens, living rooms, or other common areas. Examples include:

- **Lemon**
- **Orange**
- **Grapefruit**
- **Lime**
- **Bergamot**

95

Citrus oils are known for their cleansing properties and are ideal for removing strong odors.

3. Spicy Scents

Spicy oils are warm, stimulating, and comforting. They evoke feelings of warmth and can add depth to blends. These oils are often used for fall and winter blends or for creating cozy atmospheres. Examples include:

- **Cinnamon**
- **Clove**
- **Nutmeg**
- **Ginger**
- **Pepper**

Spicy oils work well in combination with woodsy or citrus scents.

4. Woody Scents

Woody oils are grounding, calming, and earthy. These oils are often used for creating a tranquil, zen-like environment. Examples include:

- **Sandalwood**
- **Cedarwood**
- **Pine**
- **Vetiver**

Woody oils are ideal for spaces where you need to create a peaceful, relaxing atmosphere.

5. Herbal Scents

Herbal oils are fresh and invigorating, often carrying medicinal or healing properties. They can be used to stimulate the mind and promote clarity. Examples include:

- **Peppermint**
- **Basil**
- **Rosemary**
- **Thyme**

Herbal oils are perfect for kitchens or study rooms where focus and concentration are important.

6. Sweet Scents

Sweet essential oils are rich and comforting, often associated with relaxation and indulgence. These scents can help create a warm, inviting atmosphere in any room. Examples include:

- **Vanilla**
- **Tonka Bean**
- **Cocoa**
- **Benzoin**

Sweet scents are wonderful for bedrooms and living rooms, particularly if you're aiming for a cozy, nurturing environment.

Adjusting Fragrance Strength

Once you understand the basic scent profiles, you can begin experimenting with different combinations to adjust the **strength** of your fragrance. Here are a few tips for customizing your spray's strength:

1. **More Subtle Fragrance:**

    - **Use Fewer Drops**: If you prefer a lighter scent, reduce the number of essential oil drops in your recipe. A subtle fragrance will linger in the air but won't overwhelm the space.
    - **Dilute More**: Add a bit more water or witch hazel to your mixture to dilute the essential oils further, creating a more gentle fragrance that won't be overpowering.
    - **Focus on Lighter Oils**: Citrus and floral oils tend to have a more subtle presence. You can balance out stronger scents with these oils to create a delicate blend.

2. **Stronger Fragrance:**

    - **Add More Drops**: For a more robust and long-lasting scent, you can increase the number of drops of your chosen essential oils. Keep in mind that some oils, like **peppermint** and **cinnamon**, are more potent than others, so be cautious when increasing the quantity.
    - **Use a Combination of Stronger Oils**: Spicy and woody oils tend to have stronger, more assertive fragrances. Combine them with floral or citrus oils for a more noticeable scent.
    - **Use a Smaller Bottle**: A smaller spray bottle with the same amount of essential oils will create a stronger fragrance concentration.

Creating Seasonal Blends

The scent of your room spray can reflect the **seasonal atmosphere**. You may want different fragrances during the winter months than in the summer, or even switch scents for various holidays or occasions. Here are some seasonal suggestions:

Fall/Winter Blends:

- **Cozy Cinnamon & Clove**: Perfect for creating a warm, spicy atmosphere during the colder months.
- **Woodsy Evergreen & Bergamot**: A combination of woodsy and citrus notes evokes the scent of a freshly cut Christmas tree.
- **Vanilla & Nutmeg**: A sweet and comforting blend that brings a sense of warmth and holiday cheer to your home.

Spring/Summer Blends:

- **Citrusy Lemon & Basil**: A refreshing and uplifting scent that mimics the bright and zesty vibes of spring.
- **Lavender & Mint**: A cool, calming scent perfect for warm summer evenings.
- **Peppermint & Rosemary**: Energizing and fresh, this blend is ideal for warm, sunny days.

Holiday Blends:

- **Gingerbread Spice**: Cinnamon, clove, nutmeg, and ginger create a warm, festive atmosphere that reminds you of holiday baking.
- **Frankincense & Myrrh**: An earthy and resinous blend with a deep, spiritual scent for

creating a sacred, peaceful environment during the holidays.

Customizing for Different Rooms

You can tailor your room sprays for specific rooms in your home by adjusting the scents to suit the needs of the space:

For the Kitchen:

- **Citrusy, Fresh Scents**: Citrus oils like lemon, lime, and grapefruit are excellent at neutralizing food odors while refreshing the air. You can also add a touch of **rosemary** or **basil** for a more herbal scent that complements cooking.

For the Living Room:

- **Balancing, Inviting Blends**: A combination of **lavender**, **orange**, and **frankincense** creates a balanced, inviting atmosphere. This blend can be both calming and energizing, making it perfect for spaces where you entertain guests or relax with family.

For the Bathroom:

- **Crisp, Clean Fragrances**: **Tea tree**, **lemongrass**, or **eucalyptus** are great for bathrooms as they not only provide refreshing, clean aromas but also have natural antibacterial properties to eliminate unwanted odors.

For the Bedroom:

- **Relaxing, Calming Blends**: **Lavender**, **chamomile**, and **cedarwood** are ideal for bedrooms. These oils help promote relaxation and sleep, ensuring a peaceful atmosphere for rest.

For the Office or Study Room:

- **Focus and Clarity**: **Peppermint**, **rosemary**, and **lemon** are great choices for enhancing focus and mental clarity. These oils can help invigorate your mind and boost productivity in a work or study setting.

Final Tips for Customizing Your Room Spray

1. **Start Small and Experiment**: Don't be afraid to experiment with different combinations of oils. Start with a small batch and adjust based on how you feel about the scent.
2. **Take Notes**: Keep a fragrance journal where you note down the oils you used and the results. This will help you recreate your favorite blends or improve your creations.
3. **Blend Gradually**: When experimenting with combinations, add oils gradually. It's easier to add more oil than it is to try and dilute a fragrance that's too strong.
4. **Let the Scents Evolve**: After making your room spray, let it sit for a day or two to allow the oils

to meld and develop. Sometimes a blend will smell different after it's had time to sit.

Customizing your room spray is all about experimenting with essential oils to create scents that reflect your personal preferences, mood, and the atmosphere you want to evoke. Whether you prefer the energizing freshness of citrus, the calming essence of lavender, or the warmth of cinnamon and clove, you can create a scent for every room, season, and occasion. By understanding the different scent profiles and adjusting the strength and combinations, you can craft the perfect room spray to suit your unique taste.

Experimenting with Different Combinations

Unleashing Your Creativity with Essential Oils

One of the most rewarding aspects of creating DIY room sprays is the endless opportunity for experimentation. Essential oils are highly versatile, and the combinations you can create are practically limitless. This chapter will guide you through the process of blending various oils and experimenting with new combinations to create scents that are perfectly suited to your preferences, mood, and environment.

Learning how to experiment with different combinations is not only about understanding how to mix scents, but also about discovering which aromas evoke certain feelings, enhance specific moods, and make your home more inviting. Whether you are looking for a **calming blend** for your bedroom or a **refreshing scent** for your kitchen, this chapter will show you how to mix and match essential oils to craft your own signature room spray blends.

Starting with Basic Combinations

Before diving into more complex blends, it's a good idea to get a feel for how essential oils interact. When mixing oils, there are three main approaches you can take:

1. **Single-Scent Focus**

This is the simplest approach, where you focus on one dominant scent. Using one essential oil will create a pure and straightforward fragrance. For example, **lavender** on its own can create a calming and relaxing environment, perfect for winding down in the evening.

- **Examples**:
    - **Lavender** – Relaxing and calming.
    - **Peppermint** – Refreshing and invigorating.
    - **Lemon** – Uplifting and energizing.
    - **Cedarwood** – Grounding and soothing.

2. **Complementary Blends**

Complementary blends use essential oils that naturally work well together. For example, combining **orange** with **lemon** creates a refreshing, citrusy scent that's vibrant but not overpowering. These combinations work well when you want a balanced fragrance that's easy to wear in various rooms.

- **Examples**:
    - **Lavender + Peppermint** – Calming and refreshing, ideal for relaxation.
    - **Orange + Lemon** – Uplifting and bright, great for kitchens or living rooms.
    - **Rosemary + Eucalyptus** – Clear and energizing, perfect for home offices.

3. **Layered Blends**

Layered blends involve mixing oils with different properties to create a more complex, multifaceted fragrance. For example, combining **spicy cinnamon** with **sweet vanilla** creates a rich, inviting scent that's perfect for the winter months. Layering blends can give you a fragrance that evolves as it lingers in the room.

- **Examples**:
  - **Cinnamon + Clove + Vanilla** – A warm, cozy, and comforting blend.
  - **Rose + Ylang Ylang + Patchouli** – Floral with an earthy undertone, perfect for bedrooms.
  - **Peppermint + Eucalyptus + Lemon** – Invigorating, perfect for a fresh and clean home.

Exploring Advanced Blending Techniques

Once you're comfortable with basic combinations, it's time to experiment with **advanced blending techniques**. These methods involve mixing oils from different scent families to create more dynamic and nuanced fragrances. Here are a few tips to help you craft advanced blends:

1. Combining Different Scent Families

Each essential oil comes from one of the major scent families—**citrus**, **herbaceous**, **woody**, **floral**, **spicy**, or **sweet**—and by blending oils from different families, you can create a well-rounded fragrance that feels harmonious. For example:

- **Citrus + Floral**: Combining the **freshness of citrus** with the **softness of floral** creates a light,

105

breezy fragrance that's uplifting without being overpowering. For example, **lemon + lavender** is a classic blend that's perfect for any room in your home.

- **Woody + Herbal**: A **woody + herbal** blend can create an earthy, grounding fragrance. Try **cedarwood + rosemary** or **sandalwood + sage** for a scent that's both calming and invigorating.
- **Spicy + Sweet**: Pairing **spicy** oils with **sweet** oils can create a comforting, almost dessert-like fragrance. A great example is **cinnamon + vanilla**, which evokes warmth and coziness.

2. Layering for Different Moods

Different oils have different emotional effects. Here's how you can combine scents to create mood-boosting room sprays:

- **Relaxing and Calming**: Blend **lavender + chamomile + sandalwood** for a soothing spray perfect for winding down before bed.
- **Uplifting and Energizing**: Combine **citrus oils** like **lemon** and **orange** with **peppermint** or **rosemary** for an energetic, mood-boosting spray.
- **Romantic and Inviting**: Try **ylang ylang + rose** with a hint of **vanilla** for a warm, inviting fragrance that's perfect for bedrooms or intimate settings.
- **Clean and Fresh**: A combination of **eucalyptus + lemon + tea tree** offers a crisp, refreshing scent that purifies the air and rejuvenates your space.

106

3. Adjusting for Seasonal Scents

As the seasons change, so too do the scents that feel right in your home. For example, **citrus** and **herbaceous** oils are often refreshing and invigorating, making them great for **spring and summer**, while **spicy** and **woody** oils tend to feel more comforting and cozy, perfect for **fall and winter**.

- Spring & Summer Blends:
    - **Lemon + Basil + Mint**: Crisp, refreshing, and perfect for brightening up any room.
    - **Grapefruit + Rosemary + Lavender**: Uplifting and cooling, great for the warmer months.
    - **Cucumber + Lavender + Lemon**: Clean and fresh, ideal for kitchens or bathrooms.
- Fall & Winter Blends:
    - **Cinnamon + Clove + Orange**: Warm, cozy, and comforting for cold evenings.
    - **Sandalwood + Frankincense + Myrrh**: Earthy, resinous, and calming—perfect for the holiday season.
    - **Patchouli + Cedarwood + Bergamot**: Earthy and grounding for winter nights.

Testing and Refining Your Blends

Experimenting is key to creating a room spray that's truly your own. Once you've mixed your essential oils, here's how to ensure your blend is just right:

1. Test in Small Batches

Start by making a small batch of your blend to test the fragrance. This will allow you to adjust the oils if necessary without committing to a larger amount. Mix up about 2-3 ounces of the room spray to start.

2. Let It Rest

After mixing the oils and water, allow your room spray to sit for a day or two. Sometimes, the fragrance can change and evolve as the oils combine and blend together. This resting period is important to get the true essence of your creation.

3. Fine-Tuning

After testing the scent, you may find that you want to adjust the balance. If the fragrance is too strong, add more water or witch hazel. If it's too subtle, add a few more drops of the essential oils. Don't be afraid to experiment with the ratios until you're satisfied with the outcome.

Customizing Scents for Specific Rooms

While you can use the same spray throughout your entire home, some fragrances work better in certain rooms based on the ambiance or purpose of that space.

- **Kitchen**: Fresh, citrusy scents like **lemon + peppermint** or **grapefruit + basil** work well to neutralize cooking odors while creating a fresh atmosphere.
- **Living Room**: Try **lavender + bergamot** or **orange + sandalwood** for a welcoming scent that is both relaxing and pleasant for guests.
- **Bedroom**: To promote relaxation and sleep, blends such as **lavender + chamomile + cedarwood** or **ylang ylang + rose** are perfect.
- **Bathroom**: **Eucalyptus + tea tree** or **lemongrass + lime** are clean and refreshing, making them ideal for bathrooms where you want a crisp, invigorating atmosphere.

Experimenting with different combinations of essential oils is a fun and rewarding process that allows you to tailor your room sprays to suit your personal preferences and the needs of your home. Whether you're creating a soothing, relaxing atmosphere, a fresh and invigorating environment, or a cozy and warm setting, the possibilities are endless.

Remember, there is no "right" or "wrong" when it comes to blending scents—trust your nose, and don't be afraid to explore different combinations. By testing and refining your blends, you'll discover your perfect signature scents that will make every room in your home smell just the way you want it.

Adding Natural Color and Texture (Herbs, Dried Flowers)

Enhancing Your Room Sprays with Natural Elements

In the world of DIY room sprays, the possibilities extend far beyond just scent. To elevate your homemade air fresheners even further, you can introduce **natural colors** and **textures** through the addition of herbs, dried flowers, and other plant-based elements. Not only do these ingredients enhance the visual appeal of your sprays, but they can also contribute subtle additional notes of fragrance and bring a touch of nature to your homemade creations.

By incorporating herbs and dried flowers, you can make your room sprays feel more personalized, unique, and even create blends that are visually as delightful as they are aromatic. In this chapter, we'll guide you on how to enhance your room sprays with these natural elements, ensuring your creations are both beautiful and effective.

Why Add Herbs and Dried Flowers to Room Sprays?

Incorporating herbs and dried flowers into your room sprays isn't just about looks—these natural additions serve multiple purposes. Here are a few reasons why you should consider adding herbs and dried flowers to your DIY room sprays:

1. Aesthetic Appeal

Dried herbs and flowers can give your room spray bottles a rustic, charming look. Imagine a bottle with **lavender sprigs**, **rose petals**, or **rosemary twigs** floating inside, providing a sense of tranquility and beauty even before the spray is used. The visual texture of dried flowers adds a touch of elegance to your room sprays, making them perfect for gifts or decorative items in your home.

2. Gentle Fragrance Enhancement

While the primary fragrance of your room spray will come from the essential oils, herbs and dried flowers can impart subtle notes of scent. For example, adding **lavender buds** to your spray can enhance the lavender fragrance, while **rose petals** will add a delicate, sweet floral note to complement any other scents in the blend.

3. Therapeutic Benefits

Many dried flowers and herbs have their own therapeutic properties, which can further enhance the purpose of your room spray. For instance:

- **Lavender**: Known for its calming and relaxing effects, it can help with stress relief.
- **Rosemary**: Often used to improve mental clarity and focus.
- **Chamomile**: Known for its soothing properties, making it ideal for bedrooms or spaces where relaxation is important.

- **Peppermint**: Invigorating and refreshing, perfect for a morning boost.

4. Eco-Friendly and Sustainable

Using dried flowers and herbs is a more **sustainable and natural approach** compared to synthetic additives. Dried plant materials are biodegradable, unlike some commercial air fresheners that may contain non-renewable ingredients or packaging.

Choosing the Right Herbs and Flowers for Your Room Spray

Not all herbs and dried flowers are suitable for use in room sprays, especially since some can deteriorate or lose their scent over time. Here are some of the best options to consider when enhancing your DIY room sprays:

1. Lavender

- **Properties**: Calming, relaxing, and soothing.
- **Uses**: Ideal for bedrooms, bathrooms, or any space where relaxation is desired. Adds a gentle floral note to room sprays.
- **How to Use**: Use dried lavender buds or sprigs. You can place them directly in the spray bottle or infuse them in the water for a stronger scent.

2. Rose Petals

- **Properties**: Romantic, sweet, and uplifting.
- **Uses**: Perfect for living rooms, bedrooms, or areas where you want to create a warm, welcoming atmosphere.
- **How to Use**: Dried rose petals are great for adding color and fragrance. Use them in the bottle to infuse the spray, or place them inside the cap for added texture.

3. Rosemary

- **Properties**: Refreshing, purifying, and invigorating.
- **Uses**: Great for kitchens, offices, or any area where you want to feel energized and focused. Rosemary also helps with clearing the air.
- **How to Use**: Fresh or dried rosemary sprigs can be added to your bottle. Its robust scent will infuse into the spray and also contribute a lovely texture.

4. Chamomile

- **Properties**: Soothing, calming, and gentle.
- **Uses**: Ideal for bedrooms or nurseries to promote sleep and relaxation. Chamomile's sweet floral scent pairs well with lavender or rose.
- **How to Use**: Use dried chamomile flowers to add texture and an additional calming fragrance to your spray.

5. Hibiscus

- **Properties**: Floral, fruity, and bold.
- **Uses**: Hibiscus petals provide a tropical feel and can enhance your room spray's appearance. It pairs well with citrus oils or tropical blends.
- **How to Use**: Add dried hibiscus flowers for a burst of color and a delicate fruity fragrance.

6. Peppermint Leaves

- **Properties**: Refreshing, cooling, and energizing.
- **Uses**: Perfect for kitchens, bathrooms, or workspaces. Peppermint leaves add a sharp, crisp note to your blend.
- **How to Use**: Use fresh or dried leaves and add them directly to your bottle. The leaves will release a cooling fragrance, especially in the warm months.

7. Jasmine

- **Properties**: Sweet, floral, and sensual.
- **Uses**: Best for bedrooms, bathrooms, or creating a romantic atmosphere. Jasmine enhances any blend that's floral or sweet.
- **How to Use**: Dried jasmine flowers can be added to your spray bottle for both visual appeal and a subtle sweet fragrance.

How to Incorporate Herbs and Dried Flowers into Your Room Sprays

Now that you know which herbs and dried flowers to use, it's time to explore how to incorporate them into your room sprays.

1. Infusion Method

- The infusion method involves steeping the herbs or flowers in the **liquid** before using them in your spray. This method allows the oils from the plants to blend with your base liquid (such as water or witch hazel), giving your spray a stronger, more aromatic fragrance.
- To infuse, simply place your dried flowers or herbs into the spray bottle, add the base liquid (water or witch hazel), and let it sit for **24–48 hours**. The longer the herbs sit in the liquid, the stronger the fragrance.

2. Direct Placement

- If you prefer to see the herbs or flowers floating inside your room spray bottle, you can place them directly inside. Just be sure to use **dried** herbs or flowers, as fresh materials can create moisture that could lead to mold or mildew over time.
- For a visual effect, place a sprig of **lavender**, a few **rose petals**, or a **rosemary sprig** in your bottle. As you shake the bottle, the herbs will move around, creating a visually appealing display while adding texture and color.

3. **Herbal Oil Infusion**

- Another method is to **infuse your essential oils** with herbs or flowers before adding them to your spray. This can be done by steeping herbs like **rosemary** or **lavender** in a neutral oil (like **almond oil** or **jojoba oil**) for 1–2 weeks. After the herbs have infused, strain the oil and add a few drops to your room spray.
- The infusion of oils will provide a more potent herbal fragrance while giving your spray an added depth of texture and scent.

Creating a DIY Herb and Flower Room Spray Recipe

Here's a simple recipe to help you start experimenting with adding herbs and dried flowers to your room sprays:

Lavender & Rose Petal Room Spray

Ingredients:

- 10 drops **lavender essential oil**
- 5 drops **rose essential oil**
- 1 tablespoon **witch hazel** or **vodka** (to help the oils blend with the water)
- ½ cup **distilled water**
- 2 tablespoons **dried lavender buds**
- 2 tablespoons **dried rose petals**

Instructions:

1. In a clean spray bottle, add the **lavender essential oil, rose essential oil**, and **witch hazel**.
2. Add the **distilled water** and shake well to combine the ingredients.
3. Add the **dried lavender buds** and **rose petals** to the bottle.
4. Let the spray sit for **24 hours** to allow the herbs and oils to infuse.
5. Shake before each use and spray around your room for a soothing, floral atmosphere.

Caring for Your Herbal & Floral Room Spray

To ensure your DIY room spray lasts as long as possible, follow these care tips:

- **Store in a Cool, Dark Place**: Keep your sprays away from direct sunlight or heat, as this can degrade the quality of the essential oils and herbs.
- **Use Dried Herbs Only**: Fresh herbs can cause mold or mildew to form inside the spray bottle. Always use thoroughly dried herbs or flowers.
- **Shake Before Use**: Natural additives like herbs or flowers may settle at the bottom of the bottle. Shake it gently before each use to mix the ingredients well.

Adding herbs and dried flowers to your DIY room sprays brings a new level of creativity and functionality to your creations. Not only will these additions enhance the **visual appeal** and **fragrance** of your room sprays, but they can also contribute beneficial properties that enhance your mood, health, and overall environment.

Chapter 6

Tips for Long-Lasting Scents

How to Make Your Room Spray Last Longer

One of the key benefits of homemade room sprays is their ability to create a customized atmosphere in your home. However, one challenge that often arises is ensuring that the beautiful scent of your spray lingers long enough to enjoy. Whether you're crafting a relaxing lavender mist for your bedroom or a fresh citrus spray for the kitchen, it's important to know how to make your room sprays last longer.

In this chapter, we'll explore practical tips, ingredients, and techniques that will help you extend the life of your room sprays, ensuring that the fragrances stay vibrant and pleasant for hours—or even days.

1. Choose the Right Base Ingredients

The base of your room spray plays a crucial role in how long the scent lasts. When crafting your DIY spray, it's important to choose the right ingredients to **anchor** the fragrance and ensure it sticks around longer. Below are some helpful tips:

A. Use Alcohol or Witch Hazel as a Base

- Alcohol (vodka or rubbing alcohol) and **witch hazel** are both great choices for the base of your room spray. Both of these ingredients help essential oils mix well with water while also acting as natural preservatives. Alcohol, in particular, can help **extend the life of the fragrance** by dispersing the oils and keeping them suspended in the water for longer periods of time.
- Witch hazel works similarly but also has additional **antiseptic properties**, which can be beneficial for keeping your spray free from bacteria or mold over time. It's less potent than alcohol but still effective for enhancing longevity.

B. Use Distilled Water

- **Distilled water** is essential for maintaining the quality of your room spray. Tap water may contain impurities or minerals that can cause mold or degrade the scent faster. **Distilled water** ensures your spray is clean and helps preserve the scent by not introducing unnecessary elements that could alter the fragrance over time.

---

2. Add Fixatives to Enhance Longevity

In the world of perfume-making, **fixatives** are substances that slow the evaporation of fragrance and allow scents to last longer. You can use natural fixatives in your DIY room sprays to achieve a longer-lasting fragrance. Here are a few to consider:

A. Glycerin

- **Vegetable glycerin** is a natural, non-toxic ingredient that can help prolong the fragrance in room sprays. When mixed with water, glycerin helps retain moisture and acts as a **humectant**, which attracts and holds water molecules, thus holding the scent longer in the air. It's a great way to extend the life of lighter scents, such as citrus or floral notes.

B. Sandalwood or Cedarwood Essential Oil

- **Woodsy oils** like **sandalwood** or **cedarwood** are known for their ability to act as fixatives. These oils have a rich, grounding scent and can help **anchor lighter essential oils**, making the fragrance last longer in the room. Adding just a few drops of these oils to your blend can create a more lasting scent experience.

C. Orris Root Powder

- **Orris root** is derived from the iris flower and is often used in high-end perfumery as a natural fixative. It has a powdery, floral scent and can help extend the fragrance life of your room spray. Simply add a small amount of orris root powder to your room spray mixture and allow it to sit for a day or two to infuse the fragrance.

3. Store Your Room Spray Properly

Proper storage can play a significant role in maintaining the integrity of your room spray's scent. Here are a few guidelines to keep your spray smelling fresh:

A. Store in Dark, Cool Places

- **Light** and **heat** can break down essential oils and cause the fragrance to fade more quickly. Always store your room spray in **dark glass bottles** to protect it from sunlight. If you prefer to use clear bottles for aesthetic reasons, store them in a **dark cabinet** or closet. Keeping the spray at a stable, cool temperature will help preserve its fragrance.

B. Use Airtight Containers

- Ensure that your room spray bottles are **airtight**. Exposure to air can lead to **oxidation**, which will cause the essential oils to lose their potency over time. Airtight containers ensure that the spray stays sealed and the fragrance is kept fresh for a longer period.

4. Shake Well Before Each Use

When you first make your room spray, all the ingredients may mix together perfectly. However, over time, the essential oils may begin to separate from the water and alcohol. To ensure that the fragrance is evenly distributed every time you use the spray, give the bottle a **gentle shake** before each use. This will **recombine the**

oils with the other ingredients, ensuring a fresh and strong scent each time you spray.

5. Use Less Water, More Essential Oils

While the water base in your room spray is essential for creating the liquid form, the **concentration of essential oils** directly affects how long the scent will linger. If you want your room spray's fragrance to last longer, consider adjusting the ratio of essential oils to water.

A. Essential Oil Concentration

- While a typical recipe calls for **20-30 drops** of essential oils per 1 cup of water, you can increase this concentration to give your spray a more lasting power. Adding an extra **5-10 drops** per cup of water can help intensify the fragrance and make it last longer in the room.

B. Stronger Fragrances

- Some essential oils are naturally stronger and last longer than others. For instance, **sandalwood**, **patchouli**, and **frankincense** are long-lasting scents that can hold up for hours, while **citrus** oils like lemon and orange may dissipate faster. Experiment with combining **stronger oils** to help extend the longevity of your blend.

6. Choose the Right Environment for Use

The **environment** in which you use your room spray can also impact how long the fragrance lasts. To get the most out of your spray, consider the following factors:

A. Spray in Small Doses

- Instead of using multiple spritzes of the spray all at once, try using just one or two spritzes and let the fragrance gradually fill the room. **Over-spraying** can dilute the scent and make it evaporate faster.

B. Airflow Considerations

- Strong drafts or fans can cause fragrances to dissipate quickly. It's best to use room sprays in spaces where there is minimal airflow, like bedrooms or living rooms, to ensure that the scent lingers in the air longer.

C. Use Room Sprays When the Room is Still

- If you're using a room spray to freshen up a space, do it **before** the room is actively being used. The more still the air is when you spray, the longer the scent will linger. You can also spray your room early in the day or the night before so the fragrance can settle in without being disturbed by activity.

7. Avoid Common Mistakes That Shorten the Life of Scents

There are a few common mistakes that can reduce the life of your DIY room spray scent. Avoid these to get the most out of your sprays:

A. Using Too Much Water

- Adding too much water can dilute the essential oils and weaken the fragrance. Stick to the recommended ratios to maintain the potency of the oils.

B. Not Using a Fixative

- Skipping the addition of fixatives can result in scents that fade quickly. Always use a fixative, especially when working with lighter, more volatile oils like citrus or floral scents.

By following these simple tips, you can ensure that your DIY room sprays have **long-lasting scents** that continue to freshen and beautify your home for hours. With the right combination of ingredients, proper storage, and thoughtful application, you'll be able to enjoy your favorite fragrances every day. So, experiment with different techniques, find what works best for you, and transform your home into a fragrant haven that lasts.

Storage and Care for Homemade Sprays

How to Properly Store and Maintain Your DIY Room Sprays

Homemade room sprays are a wonderful way to freshen your living spaces with custom fragrances, but to keep them effective and long-lasting, proper **storage** and **care** are essential. The ingredients you use, including essential oils, alcohol, and water, require specific conditions to maintain their potency and ensure the spray stays fresh for as long as possible. Improper storage can lead to the degradation of your oils, fading fragrances, or even the growth of bacteria or mold.

In this section, we will explore the best practices for storing your DIY room sprays and offer tips on how to extend their shelf life. This way, you can enjoy your sprays at their best for weeks—or even months—after you've made them.

1. Store Your Room Sprays in Dark Glass Bottles

Why Use Dark Glass Bottles?

- The **quality** and **potency** of essential oils can be easily damaged by exposure to light. Over time, **sunlight** and **UV rays** break down the delicate

compounds in essential oils, causing them to lose their fragrance or therapeutic properties.
- Dark-colored glass bottles—**amber**, **cobalt blue**, or **green**—protect the contents from harmful light exposure, thus preserving the integrity of your essential oils. They also add a touch of elegance to your DIY creations!

When to Use Clear Bottles

- If you prefer clear glass bottles for aesthetic reasons, keep the bottles in a **dark cupboard** or drawer when they are not in use. Just be sure to store them away from direct sunlight, as it will diminish the strength of the fragrance over time.

Tip:

- If you're planning to store your room sprays for long periods, opt for **amber** or **cobalt blue bottles** to protect the oils inside. These bottles will block UV rays while still allowing you to see the contents.

2. Store Room Sprays in Cool, Dry Places

Temperature Considerations

- Heat can accelerate the breakdown of essential oils, so it's important to store your homemade room sprays in a **cool, dry** location. Avoid places where the temperature fluctuates, such as near windows, radiators, or in bathrooms where humidity levels can vary.

- Ideally, you should store your room sprays at temperatures between **50°F (10°C)** and **70°F (21°C)**. Too much heat can cause the oils to evaporate, making the scent fade more quickly.

Humidity Levels

- **High humidity** can encourage the growth of mold and bacteria in your spray, especially if you're using water as the main ingredient. To avoid this, always keep your bottles in dry locations like **kitchen cabinets** or **drawers**, where the air is cool and free of excess moisture.

Best Storage Areas

- **Cupboards** or **closets** are perfect for storing your sprays.
- A **cool shelf in a pantry** or an **airtight box** is also a good option. Avoid storing your room spray near any heat sources like stoves, fireplaces, or heaters.

3. Seal Your Room Sprays Tightly

Airtight Seal

- A **tight seal** is essential for keeping your homemade room sprays fresh. If the bottle isn't properly sealed, the essential oils will evaporate more quickly, reducing the effectiveness and longevity of the fragrance.
- Ensure the **spray nozzle** or **cap** is securely fastened. If the bottle has a **mist sprayer**, check that it doesn't leak to prevent evaporation.

Tip:

- Make sure there's a **rubber seal** inside the cap or spray nozzle. This will create a better seal and help reduce air exposure.

---

4. Shake Your Spray Before Each Use

Why Shake?

- Over time, essential oils will naturally separate from the water or alcohol base of your room spray, so it's important to **shake the bottle** gently before each use. Shaking redistributes the oils, ensuring an even mist with every spray.
- This is especially important for homemade sprays that use **water** as a base, since water and oil do not mix easily.

Tip:

- Store your spray in a place where you can easily remember to shake it before each use, like near your desk or by your bed. If you leave it in a dark cupboard, just take it out before spraying to give it a quick shake.

5. Use Room Sprays Within a Reasonable Time Frame

Shelf Life of Homemade Room Sprays

- Even with proper care, homemade room sprays have a **limited shelf life**. Since they are made without preservatives, the scent will naturally fade over time. In general, most DIY room sprays will last **3–6 months** if stored properly.
- The **essential oils** themselves have a longer shelf life (up to a year or more), but once they are mixed with water or alcohol, the fragrance will start to fade after a few months.

Signs Your Room Spray Has Gone Bad

- **Separation of ingredients**: If the oils have separated entirely from the water and no longer mix when shaken, the spray is likely no longer effective.
- **Rancid smell**: If your room spray develops an unpleasant or off-putting odor, it may have spoiled. This could be caused by the oils going bad or contamination from bacteria or mold.
- **Cloudiness**: If the spray becomes cloudy or there is visible growth in the bottle, discard it immediately.

Tip:

- To get the most out of your room sprays, **label your bottles** with the date they were made. This way, you'll know when to use them up or make a new batch.

6. Clean Your Spray Bottles Regularly

Why Clean Your Bottles?

- If you're reusing spray bottles, it's important to **clean them thoroughly** to prevent the buildup of residue, mold, or bacteria. Over time, some of the oils can stick to the inside of the bottle, affecting the quality of your spray.
- A quick rinse with **hot water** and a little **dish soap** will do the trick, but be sure to dry the bottle completely before refilling it with your new room spray blend.

How to Clean Your Spray Bottles

1. Empty any leftover spray solution.
2. Rinse the bottle with **warm water**.
3. Add a few drops of **dish soap** or a mixture of **baking soda** and **water** to remove any oil residue. Swish it around, and let it sit for a few minutes.
4. Rinse thoroughly, then let it dry completely before refilling with your new room spray mixture.

---

7. Consider Adding Preservatives (Optional)

Why Add Preservatives?

- If you plan to store your room sprays for an extended period of time, you might want to

132

consider adding **natural preservatives** to help prevent bacteria or mold from growing. Some options include:
- **Grapefruit seed extract**: Known for its antibacterial properties.
- **Vitamin E oil**: Acts as an antioxidant and can help preserve essential oils.
- **Leucidal Liquid SF**: A natural preservative derived from radishes that can help extend the shelf life.

Tip:

- Use preservatives sparingly and always test your spray after adding them to ensure they don't alter the fragrance or texture.

Proper **storage** and **care** are essential for maintaining the effectiveness and longevity of your homemade room sprays. By following the tips outlined in this chapter, you can ensure that your creations stay fresh and aromatic for a long time. The right storage conditions, airtight bottles, and proper cleaning habits will help preserve the quality of your sprays, allowing you to enjoy the custom scents you've crafted. Whether you're using them to freshen your home, relax after a long day, or give as gifts, taking the time to care for your room sprays ensures they continue to provide the aromatic benefits you've worked so hard to create.

Using Room Sprays to Enhance Your Environment

How Room Sprays Can Transform Your Space

Room sprays aren't just about making your home smell good—they have the power to **create an atmosphere** that suits your mood, lifestyle, and daily activities. Whether you're looking to boost your energy, promote relaxation, or refresh your living space, the right fragrance can make all the difference. In this chapter, we'll explore how room sprays can enhance various environments, from the bedroom to the kitchen, and offer practical tips on how to use them to create a welcoming, calming, or invigorating atmosphere.

1. Setting the Mood with Fragrance

Fragrance is one of the most **powerful sensory triggers** that can influence your emotions and mental state. When you spray a room with the right scent, you can influence your mood, focus, and even productivity. Different scents can elicit different emotional responses, and by understanding this, you can tailor your room sprays to enhance specific aspects of your environment.

A. Relaxing and Calming

- **Lavender**, **chamomile**, and **sandalwood** are classic scents known for their calming properties. These fragrances are perfect for spaces where you unwind and relax, such as the bedroom or a quiet reading nook.
- Try a **lavender-chamomile blend** for a soothing spray that helps you wind down after a long day. A light spritz just before bed can set the tone for a peaceful night's sleep.

B. Uplifting and Energizing

- **Citrus scents** like **lemon**, **orange**, and **grapefruit** are known to be **energizing** and **uplifting**. These fragrances work well in high-traffic areas like the living room or kitchen, where they can help invigorate your senses and refresh the space.
- A **citrus-mint** or **lemon-lavender** blend can bring a burst of energy to your mornings and clear any lingering negativity from the air.

C. Focus and Productivity

- **Peppermint**, **rosemary**, and **eucalyptus** are excellent choices for creating an environment that promotes **focus** and **mental clarity**. These scents are stimulating and work wonders in spaces where you need to concentrate, such as your office or study area.
- A **peppermint-rosemary blend** can help sharpen your focus while keeping the space feeling fresh and invigorating. A quick spritz before you sit down to work can give you the mental boost you need.

2. Creating Ambiance for Specific Rooms

Each room in your home serves a different purpose, and the fragrance you choose can help enhance that experience. Here's how you can use room sprays to **complement** the function of each space:

A. Bedroom: Rest and Relaxation

- The bedroom is a sanctuary where you go to **rest**, so creating a tranquil, soothing atmosphere is key. **Lavender**, **jasmine**, and **bergamot** are known to promote relaxation and improve sleep quality. A light mist of these calming fragrances can help ease tension and prepare your body and mind for rest.
- You can also experiment with **chamomile and sandalwood** or a **cedarwood-lavender blend** for a calming yet grounding effect. These sprays can help reduce anxiety and create an environment that promotes deep, restful sleep.

B. Living Room: Inviting and Refreshing

- The living room is where you entertain guests and relax with family. It's important to create a welcoming and comfortable ambiance. Fresh, **citrusy** scents like **lemon** or **grapefruit** can work well here, creating a bright, airy atmosphere. For a cozy vibe, you might also consider **spiced** scents like **cinnamon**, **clove**, or **vanilla**.
- Try a **citrus-vanilla blend** or **grapefruit-rosewater** for a balanced, uplifting yet cozy

136

scent that keeps the space feeling both welcoming and energetic.

C. Kitchen: Clean and Invigorating

- The kitchen is where food and flavors come together, so it's essential to maintain a clean, fresh, and often **invigorating** atmosphere. **Citrus** scents are perfect for this space because they're **fresh** and **zesty**, making them ideal for neutralizing food odors.
- **Lemon**, **lime**, and **rosemary** are all great choices for creating a fresh, clean scent in the kitchen. A **lemon-rosemary** or **lime-mint** room spray can keep the space feeling bright and invigorating while helping to neutralize lingering cooking smells.

D. Bathroom: Clean and Fresh

- Bathrooms benefit from scents that are both **clean** and **refreshing**. **Eucalyptus**, **peppermint**, and **tea tree** oils are perfect for creating a fresh, invigorating atmosphere in your bathroom. These scents also have **antiseptic** properties, which add to the cleanliness of the space.
- Try an **eucalyptus-peppermint** blend or a **citrus-mint** spray to neutralize bathroom odors and create a refreshing environment.

3. Seasonal Scents for Special Occasions

Room sprays aren't limited to everyday use. With the changing seasons, you can adjust your room spray recipes to reflect the mood and energy of the time of year.

A. Fall and Winter

- In the colder months, you might gravitate toward **warm, spicy** scents like **cinnamon**, **clove**, **nutmeg**, and **ginger**. These fragrances are comforting and cozy, making them ideal for creating a **welcoming atmosphere** during the fall and winter months.
- Try a **cinnamon-vanilla** or **clove-orange** blend for a heartwarming scent that fills your home with cozy vibes.

B. Spring and Summer

- As the weather warms up, you'll likely want to use lighter, **floral**, and **herbaceous** scents. **Lavender**, **jasmine**, and **rose** are perfect for spring and summer. These fragrances capture the essence of blooming flowers and fresh herbs.
- Try a **lavender-rose** or **jasmine-citrus** blend to bring the light, airy feeling of spring and summer indoors.

4. Using Room Sprays to Improve Air Quality

Besides enhancing the atmosphere, many essential oils have natural properties that can help improve the air quality in your home. Spraying these oils can purify the air, reduce airborne bacteria, and promote healthier living conditions.

A. Antibacterial and Antiviral Properties

- Essential oils like **tea tree**, **eucalyptus**, and **peppermint** have natural antibacterial and antiviral properties that can help keep your home's air fresh and clean. A simple spritz of these oils can help eliminate germs and purify the air.
- **Lemon** and **rosemary** also have **antimicrobial** properties, which help to keep spaces fresh and reduce the spread of illness.

B. Neutralizing Odors

- **Citrus oils** like **orange** and **grapefruit** are fantastic for **neutralizing odors**. They don't just mask smells but actually eliminate the molecules that cause unpleasant odors, leaving the room smelling fresh and clean.
- For spaces like the kitchen, bathroom, and even pet areas, a citrus-based spray is a great way to maintain a clean environment.

5. Enhancing Your Experience with Room Sprays

A room spray is more than just a fragrance—it's a **sensory experience** that can elevate your mood and enhance the overall feel of your home. By strategically using room sprays to match the function of each room, you can create a home environment that reflects your personality, supports your well-being, and makes everyday life just a little bit more pleasant.

A. For Meditation and Yoga

- If you have a dedicated space for **meditation** or **yoga**, adding a room spray with calming oils like **lavender, frankincense**, or **sandalwood** can enhance the relaxation experience. A light misting before or during your practice can create a serene atmosphere that supports focus and tranquility.

B. For Entertaining and Social Gatherings

- When hosting guests, a well-chosen room spray can add to the overall ambiance of the occasion. A light mist of **citrus-vanilla** or **spice-scented** spray will not only freshen the air but also create a pleasant, inviting atmosphere.

Room sprays are an excellent way to enhance the environment of your home, transforming a space with just a few spritzes. Whether you're looking to **boost energy**, **promote relaxation**, or **purify the air**, the right scent can set the perfect tone for any room. Experiment with different blends to match your mood, the season, and the specific purpose of each room. By incorporating room sprays into your daily routine, you can create an atmosphere that's welcoming, rejuvenating, and calming, turning your home into a sanctuary that reflects your personality and preferences.

Chapter 7

Eco-Friendly and Sustainable DIY Sprays

Choosing Natural Ingredients

When making your own room sprays, one of the most important decisions you'll make is the selection of ingredients. **Eco-friendly** and **sustainable** ingredients not only benefit the planet but also ensure that the room sprays you create are free from harsh chemicals that can negatively impact your health. Choosing natural ingredients gives you control over what's in your products, allowing you to make healthier, more environmentally conscious choices.

1. Essential Oils: A Natural Powerhouse

Essential oils are the cornerstone of most DIY room sprays. They not only provide wonderful fragrances but also offer therapeutic benefits, making them the perfect ingredient for natural room fresheners.

A. Why Choose Essential Oils?

- **Plant-based**: Essential oils are extracted from plants, flowers, leaves, seeds, and bark, making them **natural** and **renewable** resources.

- **Purity**: Unlike synthetic fragrances, which can be made from chemicals, essential oils are pure and untainted by artificial substances.
- **Eco-friendly cultivation**: Many essential oils are produced by sustainable farming methods. Organic or wildcrafted essential oils, in particular, come from plants grown without pesticides, ensuring minimal environmental impact.

B. Popular Eco-Friendly Essential Oils

- **Lavender**: Known for its calming effects, lavender is a versatile essential oil used in many DIY recipes. It's a sustainable crop and widely available from eco-conscious producers.
- **Lemon**: A refreshing citrus oil with cleansing properties. Lemon is typically produced in a sustainable manner, with minimal environmental impact when grown organically.
- **Peppermint**: Another popular essential oil, peppermint is both stimulating and invigorating. It's usually grown in an eco-friendly manner, often requiring less water and pesticides.
- **Eucalyptus**: Not only does it have a refreshing scent, but eucalyptus is also a renewable resource. It's grown in eco-friendly conditions and has natural antibacterial properties.

Tip: When buying essential oils, always check for certifications like organic or wildcrafted to ensure you're getting the purest, most sustainable option.

2. Carrier Oils: Supporting and Diluting Essential Oils

Carrier oils are essential in diluting potent essential oils and helping them spread more effectively in your room sprays. Choosing a **natural** and **sustainable** carrier oil ensures that your spray is eco-friendly from top to bottom.

A. Choosing the Right Carrier Oil

- **Witch Hazel**: Often used as a base in DIY sprays, witch hazel is a **natural astringent** with antibacterial properties. It's derived from the bark and leaves of the witch hazel shrub, and it's widely available in eco-friendly forms.
- **Vodka**: High-proof vodka can also be used as a base for room sprays, especially for its ability to help dissolve essential oils and its neutral scent. Choose **organic vodka** or sustainably sourced options to maintain eco-consciousness.
- **Vegetable Glycerin**: If you want to create a more hydrating room spray, vegetable glycerin is a great choice. Derived from plants, it's a natural humectant that draws moisture into the air, keeping your room fresh and pleasant.
- **Distilled Water**: Using **distilled water** as the primary liquid for your spray is both cost-effective and natural. Be sure to use water that's free from chlorine or other additives, which can affect the scent and purity of your room spray.

Tip: Whenever possible, choose certified organic carrier oils and other natural liquids to ensure your DIY spray remains eco-friendly and non-toxic.

3. Hydrosols and Floral Waters: Eco-Friendly Alternatives

For an added layer of eco-friendly ingredients, consider using **hydrosols** or **floral waters**. These are by-products of the essential oil distillation process, containing water-soluble compounds from the plants.

A. Benefits of Hydrosols

- **Environmentally Friendly**: Hydrosols are typically produced in small batches using sustainable distillation practices. They're a great way to get the benefits of essential oils while ensuring minimal waste and environmental impact.
- **Gentle and Safe**: Hydrosols are less concentrated than essential oils, making them ideal for people with sensitive skin or those who prefer a milder scent.

B. Popular Hydrosols to Use in Room Sprays

- **Rose Water**: Known for its sweet, floral aroma, rose water is a calming addition to any room spray.
- **Lavender Hydrosol**: A gentle version of lavender essential oil, lavender hydrosol is perfect for soothing and freshening up small spaces.
- **Orange Blossom Water**: Sweet and citrusy, orange blossom water adds a fresh and uplifting note to your DIY sprays.

4. Sustainable Additives and Herbs

To add texture, color, or additional therapeutic benefits to your room sprays, you might want to include natural herbs or **plant-based additives**. These can serve as decorative elements or as natural components that further enhance your room sprays' fragrance and properties.

A. Dried Herbs

- **Rosemary**, **mint**, and **lavender** are all **easy-to-grow** herbs that can be added to your spray bottles for a visual pop and extra fragrance. When choosing dried herbs, make sure they are **ethically sourced** and grown without pesticides.

B. Other Additives

- **Baking Soda**: A common natural deodorizer, baking soda can be added to your sprays to absorb odors and neutralize the air.
- **Clays**: For a more luxurious room spray, you can use **white clay** or **kaolin clay** to help suspend the oils in your spray bottle and prevent them from separating.
- **Sea Salt**: Sea salt can enhance the texture and stability of your spray, and it has natural air-purifying properties.

5. Packaging and Sustainability

Creating eco-friendly room sprays goes beyond just the ingredients. Choosing the right **packaging** is equally important in ensuring your DIY sprays are as sustainable as possible.

A. Glass Bottles

- **Glass** is a fantastic alternative to plastic because it's **reusable, recyclable**, and doesn't leach harmful chemicals into the environment. Glass bottles are available in many shapes and sizes, and you can easily repurpose old glass containers for your sprays.
- **Amber** or **cobalt blue** glass bottles are ideal for storing room sprays, as they protect the essential oils from sunlight and UV rays, ensuring the oils remain potent.

B. Eco-Friendly Labels

- Instead of using plastic labels or synthetic materials, choose **recycled paper** or **plant-based materials** for your labels. Many small businesses offer **customizable, eco-friendly labels** that you can print at home or order.

C. Refill Stations and Bulk Buying

- To further reduce waste, consider creating refillable sprays or offering **bulk buying options** for your DIY room spray ingredients. This is a great way to minimize packaging waste and encourage others to use sustainable options.

Avoiding Harsh Chemicals and Preservatives

One of the main reasons people choose to make their own room sprays is to **avoid harmful chemicals** commonly found in commercial air fresheners. By sticking to natural ingredients, you ensure that your sprays are safe for both your health and the environment.

1. Common Chemicals to Avoid in Room Sprays

A. Synthetic Fragrances

- **Synthetic fragrances** are often made from a blend of artificial chemicals that mimic natural scents. These chemicals are often listed under the term "fragrance" or "parfum" and can contain harmful substances like **phthalates**, **formaldehyde**, and **toluene**. These compounds can cause headaches, skin irritation, and other health issues.
- Always choose **pure essential oils** instead of synthetic fragrance oils. The latter can be made from petrochemicals, which are harmful to the environment and your health.

B. Preservatives and Antimicrobials

- Many commercial room sprays contain **preservatives** and **antimicrobials** to prolong shelf life. However, some preservatives like **parabens**, **phenoxyethanol**, and **triclosan** can be toxic to both humans and the environment. Opting for **natural preservatives**, like grapefruit seed extract or **vitamin E**, can help you keep your DIY sprays safe without introducing harmful chemicals.

C. Alcohols and Solvents

- While some alcohols, such as **vodka**, can be used in DIY sprays, avoid **denatured alcohol** or **solvents** found in commercial air fresheners. These chemicals can be drying and may irritate the skin, eyes, or respiratory system.

2. The Benefits of Going Chemical-Free

By using **natural ingredients** and avoiding harmful chemicals, you ensure that your room sprays are not only safer for your family but also better for the environment. Here's why:

- **Healthier**: Natural room sprays are non-toxic and free from irritants. They are safe for children, pets, and individuals with sensitivities.
- **Eco-Friendly**: Using sustainable, plant-based ingredients reduces your environmental footprint and supports eco-conscious farming practices.
- **Long-Term Benefits**: By using essential oils and natural preservatives, your sprays remain effective over time without the need for artificial chemicals.

Creating **eco-friendly** and **sustainable DIY room sprays** allows you to enjoy a fresh, fragrant home without compromising your health or the environment.

Packaging Options for Eco-Conscious DIYers

When crafting your own **DIY room sprays**, choosing the right packaging is just as important as selecting natural ingredients. The packaging not only protects your product but also reflects your commitment to sustainability and eco-conscious practices. Below are some eco-friendly packaging options for DIY room sprays that will help reduce waste and promote a more sustainable lifestyle.

1. Glass Bottles: The Sustainable Choice

Glass bottles are the **top choice** for packaging DIY room sprays, and for good reason. They offer multiple **environmental and functional benefits** that make them the most eco-friendly option available.

A. Benefits of Glass Bottles

- **Reusable**: Glass bottles are designed to last and can be reused repeatedly. After you've finished using the room spray, you can simply clean the bottle and repurpose it for future DIY projects.
- **Recyclable**: Glass is **100% recyclable**, meaning it can be recycled infinitely without losing its quality. This significantly reduces waste and environmental impact.
- **Chemical-Free**: Unlike some plastic bottles, glass doesn't leach chemicals into the liquid inside. This ensures that your DIY room spray remains free from harmful substances and retains the full potency of the essential oils.

- **Protects Ingredients**: Glass is excellent at protecting your room spray's ingredients from the damaging effects of **UV light**. This is especially important for essential oils, which can degrade if exposed to sunlight for long periods.

B. Types of Glass Bottles for Room Sprays

- **Clear Glass**: Clear glass bottles are widely available and allow you to see the contents inside. However, they should be stored away from direct sunlight to avoid UV damage to essential oils.
- **Amber Glass**: Amber bottles are an excellent choice for essential oils and DIY room sprays because they block UV rays and protect the oils from light, maintaining their therapeutic properties.
- **Cobalt Blue Glass**: Like amber, cobalt blue glass offers UV protection and adds a lovely aesthetic touch to your DIY creations. It's a popular choice for those looking to add a touch of elegance to their room sprays.

C. Where to Find Glass Bottles

- Many **eco-conscious retailers** and bulk suppliers offer glass spray bottles, typically made from recyclable or recycled glass. You can find these bottles in various sizes and shapes, from small travel-sized spritzers to larger bottles for home use.
- **Repurposing glass containers**: If you have old glass containers such as perfume bottles, old spritzers, or even mason jars, consider **reusing** them. This cuts down on waste and gives a

second life to glass that might otherwise be discarded.

2. Aluminum Bottles: Durable and Recyclable

Aluminum is another sustainable packaging option for your DIY room sprays. It is lightweight, durable, and highly recyclable, making it an eco-friendly alternative to plastic bottles.

A. Benefits of Aluminum Bottles

- **Recyclability**: Aluminum is **100% recyclable** and can be recycled indefinitely. The recycling process for aluminum is less energy-intensive than for many other materials, reducing its carbon footprint.
- **Durability**: Aluminum bottles are **lightweight** yet sturdy, making them ideal for travel or on-the-go use. They can withstand bumps and drops, ensuring your DIY room spray stays safe.
- **Non-Toxic**: Unlike plastic, aluminum is a **non-toxic** material and doesn't leach harmful chemicals into its contents, making it safe for both the environment and your health.
- **Effective Barrier**: Aluminum is effective at keeping light and air out, which helps maintain the **freshness** of your room spray, particularly if it contains essential oils that could degrade with light exposure.

B. Types of Aluminum Bottles

- **Opaque Aluminum Bottles**: These bottles are ideal for DIY room sprays with essential oils since they block out UV light and keep the contents protected. They're available in various shapes and sizes, including small bottles for portable use and larger bottles for home use.
- **Clear Aluminum Bottles**: While still durable, these bottles do not offer the same level of protection from light as opaque options. They are best used for products that will be stored away from sunlight.

C. Where to Find Aluminum Bottles

- Many eco-friendly suppliers, including bulk retailers and specialty packaging stores, offer a variety of aluminum bottle sizes for DIY projects. Ensure that you choose bottles that are **certified recyclable** to guarantee they are truly eco-friendly.

3. Recycled Plastic Bottles

While **glass** and **aluminum** are the most sustainable choices, recycled plastic can also be a good option if you are careful about its source and use. It's essential to **prioritize bottles made from recycled plastic** over new plastic, as this helps reduce overall plastic production and waste.

A. Benefits of Recycled Plastic Bottles

- **Recycling**: Using recycled plastic helps reduce the amount of **virgin plastic** produced and supports the recycling industry. By purchasing recycled plastic products, you're helping close the loop in the recycling process.
- **Lightweight**: Recycled plastic bottles are **lightweight** and can be ideal for shipping or travel purposes. Their lightweight nature helps lower transportation costs and energy consumption.
- **Affordable**: Recycled plastic bottles are often more affordable than glass or aluminum options, making them a cost-effective choice for large-scale DIY projects.

B. Where to Find Recycled Plastic Bottles

- Look for packaging suppliers who offer **post-consumer recycled (PCR)** plastic bottles, which are made from recycled plastic products. This is a great way to reduce plastic waste without contributing to new plastic production.
- Some companies even offer **refillable plastic bottles** made from recycled materials, encouraging customers to reuse the bottles rather than disposing of them after one use.

4. Sustainable Labeling Options

Once you've selected your packaging, it's time to consider the **labels** that will help identify your DIY room spray. Eco-conscious labeling can enhance the overall sustainability of your project.

A. Paper-Based Labels

- **Recycled Paper**: Choose **recycled paper** for your labels, which reduces the need for new resources and minimizes waste. Recycled paper is widely available and can be printed using **soy-based inks**, which are non-toxic and more environmentally friendly than conventional inks.
- **Seed Paper**: If you want to go a step further, consider using **seed paper** for your labels. This paper is embedded with seeds that can be planted once the label is removed, making it a unique and environmentally friendly packaging option.

B. Water-Based Adhesives

- Choose labels that use **water-based** or **plant-based adhesives** instead of plastic-based adhesives, which can contribute to non-recyclable waste. These adhesives are biodegradable and better for the environment.

5. Other Eco-Friendly Packaging Ideas

For a truly eco-conscious approach to packaging your DIY room sprays, consider some of these alternative packaging ideas:

A. Cloth Bags or Pouches

- You can package your room sprays in **reusable cloth bags** or **pouches** made from natural fibers like cotton or linen. These can be custom printed or stamped with your logo and reused by customers or as gifts.

B. Wooden Caps

- If you're using glass or aluminum bottles, consider adding **wooden caps** to your packaging. These can be sourced from sustainable forests and give your DIY sprays a natural, rustic feel. Wooden caps are also biodegradable and more eco-friendly than plastic caps.

6. Tips for Sustainable Packaging Practices

- **Buy in Bulk**: Purchasing packaging materials in bulk helps reduce waste and packaging costs.
- **Repurpose**: Whenever possible, **repurpose** containers you already have at home to package your DIY sprays. This will help you avoid purchasing new materials and reduce your environmental footprint.
- **Offer Refills**: To minimize waste, consider offering **refill options** for your room sprays. Encourage customers or friends to bring their old bottles for refills, further reducing single-use packaging.

When creating your eco-friendly DIY room sprays, the packaging you choose plays a significant role in maintaining sustainability. Opt for **glass**, **aluminum**, or **recycled plastic** bottles, and enhance your packaging with natural and recyclable labels. By making conscious packaging decisions, you can reduce your environmental impact and share your sustainable creations with others in a meaningful way.

Chapter 8

Troubleshooting Common Issues

Why Your Spray Isn't Lasting Long

One of the most common frustrations when creating your own DIY room sprays is when the scent fades too quickly, leaving your space feeling less fresh than expected. While the art of making room sprays is relatively simple, achieving that perfect balance of long-lasting fragrance requires a bit of know-how and attention to detail. Let's explore the possible reasons why your spray isn't lasting long and how you can solve this issue.

1. Incorrect Ratio of Essential Oils to Carrier Liquid

One of the most significant factors in the longevity of your room spray is the **ratio of essential oils to carrier liquid**. Too little essential oil, and the fragrance won't be potent enough to last. Too much, and the scent may overpower or dissipate too quickly.

A. How to Get the Right Balance

- **General Rule of Thumb**: A good starting point is to use **10-20 drops** of essential oil per ounce of carrier liquid (water or witch hazel). This can be adjusted based on personal preference and the type of essential oils used. Stronger oils, like

158

eucalyptus or peppermint, may require fewer drops, while milder oils like lavender may need a bit more.
- **Tip**: If you find that your spray fades quickly, increase the number of essential oil drops or try a more concentrated carrier liquid like **vodka** or **witch hazel**, both of which help preserve the scent longer compared to plain water.

2. Using the Wrong Carrier Liquid

The choice of **carrier liquid** can greatly impact the performance and lasting power of your room spray. Some liquids evaporate faster than others, causing the fragrance to dissipate quickly. While water is the most common choice, it's not always the best for preserving the fragrance.

A. Why Water Might Not Be Enough

- **Water evaporates quickly** and doesn't hold the essential oils as effectively as other liquids. While it's still useful, it can lead to a less enduring scent.

B. Alternative Carrier Liquids to Consider

- **Witch Hazel**: Witch hazel acts as a natural preservative and can help **bind** the essential oils to the water, prolonging their scent. It also works as an antiseptic and gives your spray a cleaner feel.
- **Vodka**: Though not the most common, **vodka** is an excellent choice for a room spray base because it helps dissolve essential oils more

effectively and keeps the scent lasting longer. It also dries quickly without leaving any sticky residue.
- **Glycerin**: A small amount of **glycerin** can help slow down the evaporation process and extend the life of the scent in your spray.

3. Exposure to Heat and Sunlight

If your room spray is not stored properly, the scent can degrade much faster than expected. **Heat** and **sunlight** are two major culprits in breaking down essential oils and reducing the longevity of your fragrance.

A. Why Heat and Sunlight Matter

- **UV rays** from sunlight can break down the chemical compounds in essential oils, causing them to lose their potency and scent.
- **Heat** can also cause the carrier liquid to evaporate more quickly, reducing the effectiveness of the oils and shortening the lifespan of the spray.

B. How to Protect Your Room Spray

- Store your room sprays in a **cool, dark place** to protect them from both heat and sunlight. A cupboard, drawer, or closet is ideal.
- Opt for **dark-colored glass bottles**, like amber or cobalt blue, which help protect the oils from UV rays.

4. The Wrong Type of Essential Oils

Not all essential oils are created equal when it comes to their ability to last in a room spray. Some oils have a **lighter scent** that tends to evaporate more quickly, while others have a **heavier, more lingering fragrance**. If you're using oils with shorter evaporation times, it's no surprise that your scent doesn't last long.

A. Essential Oils That Evaporate Quickly

- **Citrus oils** (e.g., lemon, orange, lime) are known for their **bright but short-lived** scent. They tend to dissipate very quickly, leaving your space smelling fresh initially but fading soon after.
- **Herbaceous oils** like **lavender** and **peppermint** can also fade faster, although they are usually longer-lasting than citrus oils.

B. Essential Oils That Last Longer

- **Base notes**, such as **cedarwood, sandalwood, patchouli**, and **vanilla**, have a much slower evaporation rate. These oils tend to last longer, providing a more **enduring fragrance**.
- **Woody** and **spicy oils** such as **cinnamon, clove**, and **frankincense** are also known for their lasting power.

C. Blending Oils for Longevity

- To create a more balanced and long-lasting fragrance, **blend lighter oils with heavier oils**. For example, combining **citrus oils** with **woody or spicy oils** can create a fragrance that **starts fresh** but lasts longer.

- Using a combination of top, middle, and base notes in your room spray will give the fragrance more **depth and duration**.

---

5. Overuse of Fragrance

It may seem counterintuitive, but **too much fragrance** in your room spray can actually cause the scent to **fade quicker**. When you use an excessive amount of essential oils, the room spray can become **overpowering**, causing your nose to adjust to the strong scent, making it less noticeable over time.

A. How Overuse Affects Longevity

- Overusing essential oils can lead to **evaporation** of the fragrance faster than usual, as your body may acclimate to the strong scent, reducing your perception of its presence.
- Stronger oils can also **overwhelm** the carrier liquid, causing the scent to dissipate in unpredictable ways.

B. Finding the Right Scent Strength

- Start with a **moderate amount** of essential oil (10-20 drops per ounce) and adjust as needed based on how long the scent lasts and the strength of the oils you're using.
- Always make small batches of room spray and test them in various locations to determine how long the scent lasts before adjusting the recipe.

6. Poor Mixing Techniques

If the essential oils and carrier liquid are not **properly mixed**, it can result in uneven distribution of the oils, which may lead to a **weak or inconsistent scent**. The oils may also **separate** from the liquid over time, causing them to evaporate more quickly.

A. Tips for Proper Mixing

- When mixing essential oils with carrier liquids, it's best to **shake** the bottle well before each use. This ensures that the oils are properly distributed throughout the solution.
- If you find that the oils are not mixing properly with the liquid, consider using a **small amount of emulsifier** like **vodka** or **witch hazel**, which helps bind the oils to the water and prevents separation.

7. The Scent Isn't Strong Enough

Sometimes, the room spray may not be strong enough to fill the room or last for a significant period. This could be due to a **too-weak scent blend** or an **improper essential oil-to-liquid ratio**.

A. Increasing Scent Intensity

- **Add more essential oils** (but not too much, as discussed earlier) to increase the fragrance strength.

- **Choose more potent oils** like **rose, jasmine, or ylang-ylang** to provide a stronger, more prominent scent.
- **Consider adding a touch of alcohol** (like vodka) to boost the fragrance and help it last longer, as alcohol allows the scent to **linger** in the air.

A room spray that doesn't last as long as expected can be frustrating, but with a little troubleshooting and adjustment, you can enjoy **long-lasting fragrance** throughout your home. Pay attention to your choice of **essential oils**, **carrier liquids**, and **mixing techniques** to ensure your spray stays fresh and effective. Additionally, proper **storage** and choosing **the right packaging** can go a long way in extending the life of your DIY room spray. Keep experimenting, and soon you'll have a signature scent that fills your home for hours.

Fixing Overpowering Scents

Creating a perfectly balanced room spray is an art, but sometimes, the fragrance can become overwhelming or too strong, especially when using potent essential oils. An overpowering scent can be unpleasant and may even cause discomfort. If you find that your DIY room spray is too intense, don't worry – there are several ways to adjust the fragrance to make it more subtle and pleasant.

1. Dilution: The Easiest Fix for an Overpowering Scent

The simplest and most effective way to tame an overpowering room spray is to **dilute** it with more carrier liquid. This reduces the strength of the essential oils while maintaining the overall scent.

A. How to Dilute Your Room Spray

- **Increase the Carrier Liquid**: If your room spray is too strong, simply add more **water**, **witch hazel**, or **vodka** (depending on your recipe). This will **lower the concentration of the essential oils**, making the scent milder.
- **Test and Adjust**: Start by adding small amounts of the carrier liquid, shake well, and test the fragrance. Keep adjusting until you achieve a balanced scent strength that's pleasing to you.

B. What to Consider When Diluting

- **Essential Oil Type**: If you're using strong oils like **peppermint**, **eucalyptus**, or **cinnamon**, they tend to be more potent, and you'll need to be more careful with the amounts. Diluting will

165

help prevent the spray from becoming too overpowering.
- **Balance the Ratio**: If you dilute the room spray too much, it may lose its fragrance altogether. Make sure to find the **sweet spot** where the scent is still noticeable but not too overpowering.

2. Adjusting the Blend of Oils

Sometimes, the overpowering scent isn't about how much oil you've used but the **combination of oils** in the spray. Certain essential oils have very strong or harsh scents that can dominate the blend, making it seem overpowering. The key to balancing the fragrance is adjusting the **blend of essential oils**.

A. How to Fix the Blend

- **Reduce the Stronger Oils**: If the fragrance is too strong, reduce the amount of **top notes** (like **lemon**, **orange**, or **peppermint**) and **spicy oils** (such as **clove** or **cinnamon**). These oils tend to have a sharper, more intense scent.
- **Add Milder Oils**: Add oils with softer, more calming fragrances to balance the scent. Essential oils like **lavender**, **frankincense**, **geranium**, or **chamomile** are milder and can help tone down overpowering fragrances.
- **Use More Base Notes**: Base notes such as **cedarwood**, **sandalwood**, or **patchouli** tend to be grounding and longer-lasting, and can balance out sharp or overly sweet top notes.

166

B. Experimenting with Ratios

- A good rule of thumb is the **3:2:1 ratio**—three parts of a base note, two parts of a middle note, and one part of a top note. You can play around with these ratios to find what works best for your room spray.

3. Allowing the Spray to Settle

Sometimes, your room spray may seem overpowering right after you've made it, but after some time, the scent can mellow out and become more balanced. This is especially true when the spray has high concentrations of **top notes** like citrus or peppermint.

A. Let It Age

- **Let your spray sit for a day or two** before using it. The essential oils may need some time to blend together, and the scent could settle into a more balanced fragrance.
- If the spray is still too strong after aging, you can dilute it further or adjust the blend as needed.

B. Test and Adjust Over Time

- Always test your room spray after a few hours or a day of sitting. If you find that the scent has toned down but is still not to your liking, make small adjustments to the formula until you're happy with the result.

4. Use Less Frequent Spraying or Smaller Amounts

If the scent is overwhelming when you spray it, consider using **smaller amounts** or **spraying less frequently**. Sometimes, a few spritzes are enough to refresh a room, and using too much can lead to an overpowering experience.

A. How to Adjust Your Spraying Technique

- **Shorter bursts**: Instead of spraying continuously, give your bottle a **few quick pumps** for a more subtle fragrance.
- **Spray High and Away from the Nose**: If the scent is overwhelming when sprayed directly into the air, try spraying the room from a distance, aiming the nozzle **high toward the ceiling**. This will allow the mist to disperse more evenly throughout the room.

Adjusting for Allergies or Sensitivities

While essential oils can offer many benefits, they can also be too strong for some people, especially those with **allergies** or **sensitivities** to certain fragrances. If you or someone in your household experiences discomfort when using your room spray, there are ways to adjust the formula to make it more comfortable for everyone.

1. Identifying Potential Irritants

Certain essential oils are known to be **irritating** for some people, especially if they have sensitive skin, respiratory issues, or allergies. **Citrus oils, peppermint**, and **eucalyptus** are some of the most common triggers for people with allergies or asthma.

A. Essential Oils to Avoid for Sensitive Individuals

- **Peppermint**: Strong and intense, it can trigger headaches or respiratory discomfort.
- **Citrus Oils (Lemon, Lime, Orange)**: While refreshing, citrus oils can cause skin irritation or worsen respiratory issues in some individuals.
- **Eucalyptus**: Known for its strong scent, it can be overwhelming for those with asthma or bronchial conditions.

2. Choosing Gentle Oils

If you're making room sprays for someone with allergies or sensitivities, opt for **gentler essential oils** that are known for their soothing and calming properties.

A. Hypoallergenic Essential Oils

- **Lavender**: Lavender is one of the gentler essential oils and is often well-tolerated by those with allergies or sensitivities. It has a calming and relaxing scent.
- **Chamomile**: Both Roman and German chamomile are gentle and can be a great choice for sensitive individuals. They're soothing and

can help promote relaxation without causing irritation.
- **Frankincense**: A subtle, grounding scent that is not overpowering, frankincense is often a safe choice for those with sensitivities.
- **Rose**: Known for its delicate fragrance, rose oil is another hypoallergenic option that can be used in room sprays for those with allergies.

3. Reducing the Concentration of Essential Oils

When making room sprays for someone with sensitivities, you can reduce the overall **concentration of essential oils** in the formula. This will make the scent more subtle and less likely to cause irritation.

A. Adjusting the Ratio

- **Use fewer drops** of essential oils. Instead of the standard 10-20 drops per ounce, you can start with **5-8 drops** and increase gradually if the scent is too faint.
- **Dilute with a larger portion of carrier liquid**. This will not only make the scent less concentrated but also help avoid irritation.

4. Test the Spray on Small Areas

Before using your room spray in larger areas, it's always a good idea to test it in a small, less sensitive area to ensure it doesn't cause any discomfort.

A. Testing in a Small Room or Area

- **Spray a small amount** of your room spray in a **corner or bathroom** and observe how it interacts with the air. If you or someone else starts to feel any irritation, you can quickly open the windows and adjust the formula accordingly.
- **Test skin sensitivity**: If you're planning to use the spray on fabrics, test it on a small area of the fabric first to check for any staining or irritation.

5. Choose Natural, Non-Toxic Ingredients

For those who are highly sensitive to fragrances or chemicals, ensure that the essential oils you're using are **pure** and **natural**, free from any additives, artificial fragrances, or synthetic chemicals.

A. Use 100% Pure Essential Oils

- Choose essential oils that are **100% pure** and not diluted with fillers or synthetic additives. Look for oils that are **organic** or ethically sourced to ensure they're free from harsh chemicals.

B. Choose Non-Toxic Carrier Liquids

- Make sure your carrier liquid is non-toxic and free from any artificial fragrances. Stick to **water**, **witch hazel**, or **alcohol** that is free of added chemicals.

Fixing overpowering scents and adjusting room sprays for allergies or sensitivities requires a bit of fine-tuning, but with the right approach, you can create a room spray that's both pleasant and safe for everyone. Start by adjusting the **blend** of essential oils, **diluting** if necessary, and **choosing milder oils** for sensitive individuals. By experimenting and being mindful of fragrance strength, you can create a room spray that works for both you and your environment.

Chapter 9

Bonus Ideas for Room Spray Lovers

Creative Gift Ideas Using Room Sprays

Room sprays make for thoughtful, personalized, and fragrant gifts that everyone can enjoy. Whether you're looking for a unique gift for a loved one, a housewarming present, or a DIY treat for yourself, crafting a beautiful room spray is a simple and heartfelt way to show you care. Here are some creative and inspiring ideas for using room sprays as gifts that are sure to leave a lasting impression.

1. Personalized Scented Gift Bottles

Why settle for store-bought gifts when you can create something **unique** and **customized**? Personalized room sprays are an excellent way to show someone how much you care. You can match the scent to the person's personality, preferences, or even the season. The possibilities are endless!

A. Choosing the Perfect Scent

- **For a Friend Who Loves Relaxation**: Consider blending **lavender**, **chamomile**, and **sandalwood** for a calming and peaceful fragrance. This blend is perfect for winding down after a long day.
- **For the Energetic Soul**: A **citrus-based** spray, such as **lemon** or **orange**, combined with **peppermint** or **eucalyptus**, will create a refreshing and invigorating atmosphere, ideal for someone who enjoys an active lifestyle.
- **For the Nature Lover**: A blend of **cedarwood**, **juniper berry**, and **rosemary** evokes the scents of the great outdoors. This earthy fragrance is great for someone who loves spending time in nature.

B. Adding Personal Touches

- **Custom Labels**: Create personalized labels that include the recipient's name, a special message, or a description of the fragrance. You can also include the occasion for which the gift was made, such as "A Refreshing Gift for Your New Home" or "For Relaxing Evenings."
- **Decorative Bottles**: Choose beautiful spray bottles that reflect the personality of the recipient. You can find a variety of glass, metal, or even wooden bottles that will make the room spray feel extra special. For a rustic look, consider adding a few sprigs of dried lavender or rosemary inside the bottle for decoration.
- **Gift Wrap Ideas**: Wrap your room spray in a charming gift box or basket with some decorative tissue paper. Add a sprig of greenery

or a small dried flower tied with twine for an extra touch of creativity.

2. Aromatherapy Care Packages

Aromatherapy care packages are a wonderful way to share the healing benefits of essential oils with others. When combined with other natural wellness products, your homemade room sprays can enhance the overall experience of relaxation and self-care.

A. Essential Oils & Room Spray Pairing

- **Relaxing Care Package**: Pair a **lavender and chamomile** room spray with a few soothing **lavender sachets**, a calming **herbal tea**, and a **scented candle** for the perfect relaxation set. This makes a great gift for anyone in need of a little stress relief.
- **Energizing Care Package**: Pair an **energizing citrus** room spray with a **citrus-scented body lotion**, some **green tea** for an extra burst of energy, and a **motivational journal** for someone who loves to start their day with positivity.
- **Sleep Care Package**: Combine a **lavender or sandalwood** room spray with a soft, cozy **sleep mask**, a calming **herbal pillow spray**, and a **relaxing bath bomb** for the ultimate nighttime care package.

B. Packaging Ideas

- **Natural Baskets**: Use eco-friendly baskets made of woven jute or recycled materials. Fill them with your homemade room spray, along with other wellness products like oils, soaps, or

175

candles. Top the basket with a decorative ribbon or a handwritten note to give it a personal touch.
- **Cloth Gift Bags**: For a smaller package, try using cloth gift bags made from **organic cotton** or **hemp**. These bags are reusable and eco-friendly, which makes them perfect for a sustainable gift.
- **Glass Jars or Bottles**: For a more rustic, old-fashioned feel, package the room spray in **recycled glass jars** or **vintage-style bottles**. Add a piece of twine, a tag, or a ribbon to make it feel extra special.

3. DIY Gift Sets for Special Occasions

Room sprays are versatile enough to suit any occasion. You can create gift sets for birthdays, holidays, anniversaries, or even as **thank-you gifts** for friends and colleagues. The customization possibilities allow you to tailor the scents and themes to the recipient's preferences.

A. Holiday-Themed Gift Sets

- **Christmas**: Create a **winter-inspired** gift set with **cinnamon**, **clove**, and **pine** room spray, paired with a **festive scented candle** and a cozy blanket. This will instantly bring the warmth and comfort of the holiday season to their home.
- **Valentine's Day**: A romantic set featuring **rose**, **ylang-ylang**, and **jasmine** room spray, along with a **rose-scented body lotion** and a box of **handmade chocolates**, makes a thoughtful and sweet gift for a loved one.

- **Spring**: For a spring-themed gift set, combine **floral scents** like **rose, lavender,** and **geranium** in the room spray. Pair it with a **handmade flower bouquet** or **wildflower seed packets** for a refreshing touch of nature.

B. Wedding and Party Favors

- **Wedding Favors**: Room sprays make for elegant wedding favors. Choose a **floral fragrance** like **lily of the valley** or **peony**, and package it in delicate glass bottles with personalized labels for each guest.
- **Party Favors**: If you're hosting a dinner party or a special event, room sprays can serve as beautiful, scented takeaways. Create custom blends inspired by the theme of your party, such as **tropical scents** for a summer bash or **warm, spicy notes** for a fall gathering.

4. Aromatherapy Inhalers for On-the-Go

For those who love to carry their favorite scents with them wherever they go, an **aromatherapy inhaler** can be a perfect gift. These small, portable inhalers hold a small amount of essential oils, and you can personalize them with the same scents you use in your room sprays.

A. Creating Aromatherapy Inhalers

- **Materials Needed**: You'll need **inhaler tubes** (available online or in craft stores), **cotton wicks**, and a few drops of essential oil.

- **How to Use**: Add a few drops of your chosen essential oil blend to the cotton wick, place the wick inside the inhaler tube, and close it up. The scent will last for weeks and can be carried around easily in a purse or bag.
- **Customizing the Blends**: Create specific blends for different moods, such as a **calming blend** for stress relief or an **energizing blend** for mental clarity. Add a label to personalize each inhaler, making them a thoughtful gift for anyone who needs a little pick-me-up.

5. Room Spray Crafting Parties

For a fun, interactive experience, consider hosting a **room spray crafting party**! This can be a great activity for friends or family, and everyone can create their own personalized room spray to take home.

A. Hosting a Room Spray Crafting Party

- **Set Up a DIY Station**: Provide various essential oils, carrier liquids, and bottles for each guest. You can have a variety of scents to choose from and encourage guests to experiment with their own combinations.
- **Provide Instructions**: Create simple instructions for guests to follow, explaining how to measure the oils, mix them, and bottle their creations. You can even print out some scent combinations for inspiration.
- **Add a Fun Element**: Set up a station for labeling the sprays with personalized names or

messages. This will make the room spray more meaningful and unique to each person.
- **Party Favors**: After the crafting session, give each guest a small bottle of your own homemade spray as a party favor to remember the event.

Room sprays are not only a wonderful way to refresh your home but also an excellent opportunity to get creative with personalized gifts. Whether you're crafting a thoughtful gift for a friend, creating a DIY wellness package, or even hosting a crafting party, there are endless possibilities for using room sprays as gifts. By combining your creativity with the art of scent blending, you can make gifts that are both meaningful and memorable, leaving your loved ones with a little touch of fragrant joy.

Seasonal Variations: DIY Sprays for Holidays and Special Occasions

When it comes to creating room sprays, one of the most delightful ways to personalize them is by tailoring the scent to fit the season or special occasion. Whether you're celebrating the warmth of summer, the cozy vibes of winter, or the festive atmosphere of a holiday, the right blend of fragrances can set the mood and enhance the ambiance. In this chapter, we'll explore how to craft seasonal and holiday-inspired DIY room sprays that will not only fill your home with beautiful scents but also make for unique, thoughtful gifts.

1. Spring Scents: Fresh and Floral

Spring is all about renewal, growth, and the vibrant burst of flowers in bloom. As nature wakes up from its winter slumber, the air is filled with fresh, uplifting fragrances. Crafting a spring-inspired room spray can bring that same sense of rejuvenation to your space.

A. Classic Floral Blends

- **Ingredients**: Rose, lavender, geranium, jasmine, and ylang-ylang.
- **Scent Profile**: Light, fresh, and floral.
- **Why It Works**: These flowers bloom in the spring, and their fresh, delicate fragrances will

instantly brighten up any room. They're perfect for adding a sense of calm and peace to your home or office space.
- **Recipe**:
    - 10 drops **rose essential oil**
    - 10 drops **lavender essential oil**
    - 5 drops **geranium essential oil**
    - 1 tablespoon **vodka** or **witch hazel**
    - 3/4 cup **distilled water**
    - Shake well before each use.

B. Citrus Burst

- **Ingredients**: Lemon, orange, grapefruit, lime.
- **Scent Profile**: Fresh, zesty, and uplifting.
- **Why It Works**: Citrus oils are known for their refreshing and energizing properties. Perfect for bringing a lively and cheerful vibe to your home, they evoke the sense of a bright, sunny spring day.
- **Recipe**:
    - 10 drops **lemon essential oil**
    - 10 drops **orange essential oil**
    - 5 drops **grapefruit essential oil**
    - 1 tablespoon **vodka** or **witch hazel**
    - 3/4 cup **distilled water**
    - Shake well before each use.

2. Summer Scents: Light and Energizing

Summer is all about relaxation, outdoor fun, and warm sunshine. The right room spray can capture the essence of summer—whether you're at the beach, lounging in a garden, or enjoying a summer evening outdoors. Look for fresh, bright, and energizing scents to keep your space feeling airy and vibrant.

A. Tropical Paradise

- **Ingredients**: Coconut, lime, ylang-ylang, pineapple.
- **Scent Profile**: Sweet, fruity, and exotic.
- **Why It Works**: Tropical scents bring the feeling of a sunny beach vacation into your home. The combination of coconut and lime is especially refreshing, while the pineapple adds a juicy, sweet touch to the mix.
- **Recipe**:
    - 10 drops **coconut essential oil**
    - 10 drops **lime essential oil**
    - 5 drops **ylang-ylang essential oil**
    - 1 tablespoon **vodka** or **witch hazel**
    - 3/4 cup **distilled water**
    - Shake well before each use.

B. Fresh Mint & Eucalyptus

- **Ingredients**: Peppermint, eucalyptus, spearmint.
- **Scent Profile**: Cool, minty, and refreshing.
- **Why It Works**: This invigorating blend is perfect for hot summer days when you need a cooling, energizing spray. The peppermint and

eucalyptus combination gives the feeling of a refreshing breeze, while spearmint adds a sweet and minty touch.

- **Recipe**:
    - 10 drops **peppermint essential oil**
    - 10 drops **eucalyptus essential oil**
    - 5 drops **spearmint essential oil**
    - 1 tablespoon **vodka** or **witch hazel**
    - 3/4 cup **distilled water**
    - Shake well before each use.

3. Fall Scents: Warm and Cozy

As the days get cooler and the leaves start to change, the fall season brings a sense of warmth and comfort. Spicy, earthy, and woody scents are perfect for creating that cozy atmosphere you crave during this time of year. These fragrances are ideal for filling your home with the rich, comforting scents of autumn.

A. Spiced Pumpkin

- **Ingredients**: Cinnamon, clove, nutmeg, vanilla.
- **Scent Profile**: Warm, spicy, and sweet.
- **Why It Works**: Pumpkin is a quintessential fall scent, and when combined with spices like cinnamon and clove, it creates a cozy, inviting atmosphere. This fragrance is perfect for celebrating the harvest season or for creating a warm environment as the weather cools.
- **Recipe**:
    - 10 drops **cinnamon essential oil**
    - 5 drops **clove essential oil**

- 5 drops **nutmeg essential oil**
- 5 drops **vanilla essential oil**
- 1 tablespoon **vodka** or **witch hazel**
- 3/4 cup **distilled water**
- Shake well before each use.

B. Apple Cinnamon Delight

- **Ingredients**: Apple, cinnamon, orange.
- **Scent Profile**: Sweet, spicy, and fruity.
- **Why It Works**: Nothing says fall quite like the smell of baked apples with a dash of cinnamon. This combination creates a homely, nostalgic scent that's perfect for cool autumn evenings and festive gatherings.
- **Recipe**:
  - 10 drops **apple essential oil**
  - 5 drops **cinnamon essential oil**
  - 5 drops **orange essential oil**
  - 1 tablespoon **vodka** or **witch hazel**
  - 3/4 cup **distilled water**
  - Shake well before each use.

4. Winter Scents: Cozy and Inviting

Winter is the season for family gatherings, fireside chats, and moments of warmth and comfort. The right winter scent can fill your home with a sense of coziness and cheer, making it the perfect backdrop for holiday celebrations or simply curling up with a good book.

A. Holiday Spice

- **Ingredients**: Cinnamon, clove, orange, pine.
- **Scent Profile**: Warm, spicy, and festive.
- **Why It Works**: This classic holiday blend brings the warmth of spices and the fresh scent of pine trees into your home. It's perfect for creating a festive atmosphere during the colder months.
- **Recipe**:
    - 10 drops **cinnamon essential oil**
    - 5 drops **clove essential oil**
    - 5 drops **orange essential oil**
    - 5 drops **pine essential oil**
    - 1 tablespoon **vodka** or **witch hazel**
    - 3/4 cup **distilled water**
    - Shake well before each use.

B. Winter Wonderland

- **Ingredients**: Peppermint, vanilla, fir, and eucalyptus.
- **Scent Profile**: Cool, fresh, and comforting.
- **Why It Works**: This refreshing yet cozy blend mimics the feeling of a fresh winter morning, with the crispness of fir trees and the sweetness of vanilla and peppermint. It's perfect for adding a cozy touch to chilly winter days or holiday gatherings.
- **Recipe**:
    - 10 drops **peppermint essential oil**
    - 10 drops **vanilla essential oil**
    - 5 drops **fir needle essential oil**
    - 5 drops **eucalyptus essential oil**
    - 1 tablespoon **vodka** or **witch hazel**
    - 3/4 cup **distilled water**

- Shake well before each use.

5. Special Occasions: Scents for Celebrations

Room sprays aren't just for everyday use—they're also wonderful for adding a special touch to celebrations and milestones. Whether it's a wedding, birthday, or anniversary, you can create room sprays that perfectly complement the theme or mood of the occasion.

A. Wedding Day Bliss

- **Ingredients**: Rose, jasmine, sandalwood, lavender.
- **Scent Profile**: Floral, romantic, and uplifting.
- **Why It Works**: Weddings are often marked by romance and elegance. The combination of rose and jasmine creates a classic, loving fragrance, while sandalwood adds a warm, grounding note. Lavender brings a calming effect, making it perfect for the big day.
- **Recipe**:
    - 10 drops **rose essential oil**
    - 5 drops **jasmine essential oil**
    - 5 drops **sandalwood essential oil**
    - 5 drops **lavender essential oil**
    - 1 tablespoon **vodka** or **witch hazel**
    - 3/4 cup **distilled water**
    - Shake well before each use.

B. Birthday Bash

- **Ingredients**: Sweet orange, lavender, patchouli.
- **Scent Profile**: Sweet, uplifting, and grounding.

- **Why It Works**: This blend is perfect for birthdays as it offers both joy and relaxation. Sweet orange uplifts the spirit, lavender adds

a soothing touch, and patchouli grounds the scent with a slightly earthy base.

- **Recipe**:
    - 10 drops **sweet orange essential oil**
    - 5 drops **lavender essential oil**
    - 5 drops **patchouli essential oil**
    - 1 tablespoon **vodka** or **witch hazel**
    - 3/4 cup **distilled water**
    - Shake well before each use.

Seasonal room sprays not only help to bring the scents of nature and the festive spirit into your home, but they also make fantastic, personalized gifts for any occasion. From the floral notes of spring to the cozy spices of fall and the crisp freshness of winter, you can customize your DIY room sprays to match the mood of each season. Whether you're celebrating holidays, special occasions, or simply want to create a welcoming environment, these seasonal blends will add warmth, freshness, and joy to your space.

Making Room Spray Sets for Friends and Family

Room sprays are not only great for enhancing your home's ambiance, but they also make thoughtful and personalized gifts for friends and family. The beauty of DIY room sprays lies in their versatility. You can create custom scents that reflect the tastes and personalities of your loved ones. Whether for birthdays, holidays, housewarmings, or simply as a token of appreciation, a homemade room spray set is a unique and meaningful gift that everyone can enjoy.

In this chapter, we'll walk through how to create beautiful and fragrant room spray sets that will delight your friends and family. From selecting scents to packaging, you'll learn how to design a gift that looks as beautiful as it smells.

1. Choosing the Right Scents for Different People

When it comes to making room sprays for others, the key is personalization. Consider the recipient's tastes, lifestyle, and the type of environment they enjoy. For example, if you're making a set for someone who loves relaxation, lavender or chamomile would be ideal. On the other hand, if the person enjoys energizing scents, consider blends like citrus or peppermint. Here's how to choose:

A. For the Relaxer: Calming and Soothing Scents

- **Lavender**: Known for its calming properties, lavender is perfect for those who enjoy winding down at the end of a busy day.
- **Chamomile**: Often used in aromatherapy to relieve stress, chamomile creates a soft, floral fragrance that induces tranquility.
- **Sandalwood**: Warm, earthy, and grounding, sandalwood is ideal for those who seek comfort and calm.

Gift Idea: A relaxing set featuring Lavender & Chamomile and Sandalwood blends will offer the gift of peace and relaxation.

B. For the Energizer: Fresh and Uplifting Scents

- **Citrus**: Lemon, orange, or grapefruit bring bright, clean, and energizing aromas that will help your recipient stay alert and cheerful.
- **Peppermint**: A refreshing scent known to boost energy and improve concentration, peppermint is perfect for someone who thrives on freshness.
- **Eucalyptus**: With its crisp and refreshing qualities, eucalyptus can refresh the air and clear the mind.

Gift Idea: A rejuvenating set featuring Fresh Citrus Breeze and Eucalyptus Mint would be perfect for a morning pick-me-up.

C. For the Nature Lover: Earthy and Grounding Scents

- **Pine**: Fresh and woodsy, pine is perfect for those who love the outdoors and enjoy the scent of evergreen trees.
- **Patchouli**: With its deep, earthy aroma, patchouli is ideal for someone who appreciates a more earthy, grounding fragrance.
- **Cedarwood**: Rich and woody, cedarwood provides a sense of stability and warmth.

Gift Idea: A nature-inspired set with Pine Forest and Cedarwood & Bergamot would transport your recipient to a peaceful forest retreat.

---

2. Designing Your Room Spray Set

Once you've chosen the scents that will best suit your recipients, it's time to think about the design of the gift itself. Creating a room spray set involves more than just the sprays themselves—it's about presentation and adding a personal touch.

A. Select Beautiful Bottles

- **Glass Bottles**: Clear or frosted glass bottles add an elegant touch and showcase the beauty of your homemade room sprays. They are a more eco-friendly option and can be repurposed by the recipient after the spray is finished.

- **Colored Bottles**: If you want to create a specific vibe, you can choose colored bottles (like amber or cobalt blue) that reflect the mood of the scents inside. Amber bottles also protect essential oils from sunlight, helping to preserve the quality of your sprays.
- **Bottles with Spray Nozzles**: Make sure to select bottles that come with a fine mist nozzle to ensure that your sprays are easy to use and give off a soft, even mist.

B. Personalize the Labeling

- **Custom Labels**: You can either print or handwrite labels to give your room spray set a personal touch. Include the scent name, a short description, and any other personal message you'd like to share. Consider using calligraphy or decorative fonts for a more elegant look.
- **Label Design Ideas**: For a more rustic or natural feel, use kraft paper labels or simple white labels with minimal design. You could also create labels with floral designs, nature-inspired motifs, or something related to the recipient's personality.

C. Packaging and Presentation

- **Gift Boxes or Bags**: For a polished look, package your room spray bottles in a small gift box, decorative bag, or basket. Fill the bottom with shredded paper or a soft cloth to secure the bottles in place and add a bit of luxury.
- **Decorative Ribbons**: Add a ribbon or twine around the neck of the bottles for a rustic or chic

touch. For an even more festive look, use satin ribbons or fabric bows.
- **Accompanying Gifts**: If you want to make the gift even more special, pair your room sprays with a matching item such as a scented candle, essential oil diffuser, or a set of handmade soaps.

3. Creating a Themed Room Spray Set

Adding a theme to your room spray set can make the gift even more meaningful. Here are a few ideas for themed sets:

A. Seasonal Theme

- **Spring**: Combine floral and fresh citrus blends like Lavender & Lemon or Rose & Geranium with packaging that features floral patterns and pastel colors.
- **Fall**: Create a cozy, autumnal gift with scents like Cinnamon & Clove or Pumpkin Spice, packaged in warm tones like deep oranges, browns, and gold.
- **Winter Holidays**: For the holidays, think of spicy, sweet blends like Holiday Spice (Cinnamon, Clove, Orange) or Winter Wonderland (Peppermint, Vanilla, Fir). Package the room sprays in gift boxes with festive wrapping paper or in mason jars with a holiday ribbon.

B. Self-Care and Relaxation Theme

- Combine soothing scents like Lavender & Chamomile, Sandalwood, and Ylang-Ylang for a calming, spa-like atmosphere. You can include an additional item like a bath bomb, face mask, or a relaxing herbal tea to complete the set.
- For packaging, opt for calming shades like lavender, soft pink, or beige, and use a soft linen or cotton bag for the presentation.

C. Fresh & Clean Theme

- Choose scents like Fresh Citrus Breeze (Lemon, Orange, Lime) or Eucalyptus Mint for a fresh and clean scent. Packaging should be minimal and elegant—think clear glass bottles with clean lines and neutral-colored ribbons or twine.

4. Adding a Personal Touch

To make your room spray set even more meaningful, consider including a handwritten note or small tag. Personalize your message to let the recipient know why you chose those particular scents for them. Here are some ideas for what you could include:

- **For the Relaxer**: "I know you love a calm, soothing space to unwind after a long day. Enjoy

these scents and let them bring peace to your home."
- **For the Nature Lover**: "Inspired by the outdoors, this set brings the natural beauty of the forest and mountains right into your living room."
- **For the Energizer**: "These uplifting scents are designed to help you stay focused and energized throughout your day."

Creating room spray sets for friends and family is an excellent way to show thoughtfulness and love. By selecting the right scents, presenting them beautifully, and adding that personal touch, you can create a meaningful, customized gift that will be cherished. Whether it's for a special occasion or just because, a room spray set brings fragrance and joy into your loved ones' homes—and they'll remember your thoughtful gesture every time they spray the room. Happy gifting!

Conclusion

Enjoying a Natural, Fragrant Home Every Day

As you've discovered throughout this book, DIY room sprays offer a simple yet powerful way to enhance the atmosphere of your home naturally. Whether you're seeking relaxation, energy, or a fresh, clean environment, you now have the knowledge to create your own custom sprays that can transform any room. The beauty of DIY room sprays is that they not only elevate the air quality but also allow you to craft fragrances that suit your personal preferences, moods, and the seasons.

Making your own room sprays also aligns with a lifestyle that prioritizes eco-friendliness, sustainability, and wellness. With the simple ingredients, a bit of creativity, and a dash of patience, you can enjoy a fragrant, peaceful, and harmonious home every day without relying on chemical-laden, commercial air fresheners.

By following the tips and recipes outlined in this book, you have the ability to create a home environment that supports your health, well-being, and personal style—one spritz at a time. The therapeutic benefits of natural essential oils, combined with your own personal touch, will ensure that your home smells inviting and comforting all year round.

Final Tips for Making the Most of Your DIY Room Sprays

To get the most out of your homemade room sprays, here are a few final tips that will help you maintain their effectiveness and ensure a long-lasting, pleasant fragrance:

1. Use the Right Ratio of Ingredients

Always follow the recommended ratios of essential oils, water, and alcohol or witch hazel for optimal scent dispersion and longevity. Too much essential oil can lead to overpowering aromas, while too little can result in a faint scent. Experiment with small batches until you find your perfect blend.

2. Shake Before Each Use

Essential oils tend to separate from water, so it's important to shake your bottle before each use to re-mix the ingredients and ensure an even spray. This also helps to preserve the potency of the oils.

3. Store Sprays in a Cool, Dark Place

To preserve the integrity of your DIY room sprays, store them in a cool, dark place, away from direct sunlight. Essential oils can degrade when exposed to sunlight, so keeping your bottles in a cupboard or drawer will ensure they last longer.

4. Refresh Your Sprays Regularly

To keep your home smelling fresh, refresh your room sprays every few weeks or as the scent begins to fade. If you notice a decrease in fragrance strength, it's time to make a new batch or tweak your formula to your liking.

5. Get Creative with Seasonal Blends

Seasonal scents can make your home feel more festive and aligned with the time of year. Experiment with warm, spicy blends in the fall, floral and citrusy scents in the spring, and calming lavender and mint in the summer. Having a variety of scents to match the seasons can keep your space feeling fresh and exciting.

6. Customize Your Sprays as Gifts

As mentioned earlier, room sprays make wonderful personalized gifts. Whether for holidays, birthdays, or special occasions, you can customize your sprays to reflect the recipient's preferences. Add a handwritten note to give your gift an extra personal touch.

7. Use Your Sprays as Multi-Taskers

While DIY room sprays are ideal for freshening up a room, they can also be used in a variety of other ways:

- **As a linen spray**: Lightly spritz your bedsheets, pillows, or towels for a fresh scent.
- **As a fabric refresher**: Use on curtains, upholstery, or rugs to keep fabrics smelling clean.
- **In your car**: Keep a small bottle in your vehicle for a quick refresh while you're on the go.
- **As a shoe spray**: Eliminate unpleasant odors from shoes by spraying the inside lightly with your favorite scent.

By applying these simple yet effective tips, you'll be able to maintain a fragrant and welcoming home that reflects your personal style and preferences. With DIY room sprays, you are in control of the ingredients and fragrances, making it easy to create an environment that nurtures your body, mind, and spirit.

Thank you for joining me on this fragrant journey, and I hope you'll continue to experiment with new scents, ideas, and blends to keep your home smelling amazing every day!